THE MATHEMATICAL SUBLIME

WRITING ABOUT POETRY

Mark Scroggins

MADHAT PRESS
ASHEVILLE, NORTH CAROLINA

MadHat Press
MadHat Incorporated
PO Box 8364, Asheville, NC 28814

Copyright © 2016 Mark Scroggins
All rights reserved

The Library of Congress has assigned
this edition a Control Number of
9781941196342

ISBN 978-1-941196-34-2 (paperback)

Cover art and design by Marc Vincenz
Book design by MadHat Press

www.madhat-press.com

First Printing

For JL
again

Table of Contents

Introduction — vii

1. REVIEWS

The Condition of Hebrew: Geoffrey Hill, *Speech! Speech!* — 1
A Tinkertoy Poetics: Charles Bernstein, *All the Whiskey in Heaven* — 10
Kedging in Time: John Matthias, *Kedging* — 15
The New Colossus, Revisited: Jonathan Barron and Eric Selinger,
  Jewish American Poetry — 20
Passionate, Eccentric Reading: Norman Finkelstein,
  Not One of Them in Place — 29
By the Rivers of Babylon: Maeera Shreiber, *Singing in a Strange Land* — 33
Zuk and Ole Bill: *The Correspondence of William Carlos Williams
  and Louis Zukofsky* — 37
A Poetics of Being: Peter Nicholls, *George Oppen
  and the Fate of Modernism* — 42
Scars and Fascination: John Wilkinson, *Proud Flesh*
  and *Lake Shore Drive* — 46
Resignation and Independence: Robert Archambeau, *The Poet Resigns* — 50
Twilight Gardening: Ronald Johnson, *The Shrubberies* — 55
Postmodern Poetry's Blue Period: Rachel Blau DuPlessis, *Blue Studios* — 63
Innovation's Explainer: Peter Quartermain, *Stubborn Poetries* — 73
The Book of Oz: Ronald Johnson, *ARK* — 78

2. ESSAYS

Susan Howe's Hauntologies — 89
The "half-fabulous field-ditcher": Ruskin, Pound, Geoffrey Hill — 99
The "net / (k)not—work(s)" of Robert Sheppard's
  Twentieth Century Blues — 111
"I am not an occultist": Robert Duncan's *H. D. Book* — 121
The Master of Speech and Speech Itself: Nathaniel Mackey's
  "Septet for the End of Time" — 127

Mark Scroggins

100 Poem-Books

Introduction to 100 Poem-Books	135
100 Poem-Books	139
Index to 100 Poem-Books	199
About the Author	202

Introduction

I knew I wanted to be a writer from an early age. Precisely what sort of writer I wanted to be was another matter, one which took a good deal longer to untangle—and which I guess I'm still figuring out. When I joyfully inherited my dad's Olympia portable typewriter at eleven or twelve, I set to composing chapters of an potentially endless vampire-story, modeled in part on Stoker's *Dracula* and in part on the Victorian penny dreadful *Varney the Vampire*, which I had out from the library on seemingly permanent loan. A year or two later I fell to writing sword-and-sorcery epics, imitating the purplest passages of Robert E. Howard, Michael Moorcock, and Karl Edward Wagner. In my first years in college, as I waffled among potential majors—computer science? psychology? sociology?—before settling down with the retrospectively inevitable double major in English and philosophy, I was chipping away at a grand psychological-philosophical realist monument in the vein of Dostoevsky and (blush) John Gardner.

Poetry was always there, however. I can't remember a time when I didn't have my father's copy of *The Portable Blake* (edited by, of all people, Alfred Kazin) on my shelf, much-thumbed and much-returned to. I read and re-read *The Waste Land* in high school—and of course it wasn't on the syllabus—because I'd heard it was the craziest, most far-out thing ever written. And when I got to college, I devoured both the canonical works on the class reading lists—Donne, Shakespeare, Milton, Dickinson, Bishop, Roethke—and the tantalizing not-yet- or not-so-canonized names that I happened upon in my own reading. Eliot led to Pound; Pound led to William Carlos Williams, Charles Olson, Louis Zukofsky, Robert Creeley; and through a whole series of connections and suggestions I got to Basil Bunting, Lorine Niedecker, Jonathan Williams, Gertrude Stein, Ronald Johnson, Michael Palmer, Robert Duncan, Susan Howe, Geoffrey Hill, J. H. Prynne....

At some point I figured out that poetry was what I wanted to write. The breakthrough (if you can call it that, since I don't recall any particular road to Damascus moment) came when I realized that *writing poetry* and *being a poet* weren't necessarily the same thing, at least in my own imagination. The notion of *being* a poet was somehow too intimidating:

would I have to take on a high prophetic calling? would I have to wear turtlenecks and a beret? would I have to be able to recite my verses on demand? (One of my philosophy professors recalled introducing himself as "a philosopher" to his girlfriend's rural Virginia father; "Well then," the old man replied, "let's hear some of yer *sayin's*!")

Above all, taking on the subject-position of *the poet* seemed to me all too pretentious or presumptuous, as if by calling myself "poet" I was somehow shouldering in with Shakespeare, Keats, Dickinson, and a cloud of other worthies whose sandals I wasn't worthy to fasten. My diffidence, I suspect, had a lot to do with my fundamentalist background, a community in which one was always asking higher powers for permission to do things, and was always worried about whether one had gotten too big for one's britches.

At any rate, I did an end-run around *being* a poet by becoming a guy *who wrote* poetry. I wrote poetry as an undergraduate, and studied with the department's resident poet. But I didn't see writing poetry as a career path: I would become a professor, so I could talk *about* other people's poetry, and write my own poems on my own time. When I went to graduate school to get my PhD in literature, I finagled my way into the MFA program as well, so that I could have the time to write more poetry. Eventually, after I finished both degrees, did a stint of adjuncting, and finally got a full-time tenure-track position as a professor of literature, I found myself teaching poetry workshops and directing theses in our own MFA program. Along the way, I published some poems, found them praised by some people (and of course ignored by many more—which is after all the condition of poetry for everybody), and collected them into a few books, which got published.

Poetry was always something I wrote for myself (and of course for some real and imagined ideal audience), however: making poetry has never my central vocational activity as an academic. To be a professor of literature involves talking about poetry in front of classes, and writing about poetry. And as I discovered fairly quickly, there are a great number of ways one can write about poetry, from book-length career overviews of individual poets to three- or four-page reviews of poetry collections.

I think I've tried my hand at a wide range, from the 500-odd pages of my biography of Louis Zukofsky to the various brief thoughts on contemporary poetry I've been moved from time to time to commit to the space of my weblog.

Whatever diffidence I still feel, I guess it's pretty clear that I've achieved that original goal: I've grown up to be a writer. And the bulk of what I've written falls into two categories: poetry, and writing *about* poetry. The pieces I've gathered here are selections from the latter group: a few essays on poems and poets whose work I've found myself returning to again and again; a number of formal and informal reviews of books of poetry and poetry criticism (and one anthology that includes both poems and commentaries); and "100 Poem-Books," a marathon-like reading-through of a big chunk of—well, not exactly contemporary American poetry, or even contemporary English-language poetry, but of my "poetry to be read" shelves.

* * *

As I've said elsewhere, I find writing poetry difficult and sometimes frustrating. Writing about poetry comes somewhat more easily, but it has its own challenges. For one thing, there's so much poetry out there to read, to think about, and to write about. How in the world does one choose which poets, poems, collections of poetry to address, out of the world of stuff out there? At the beginning of his *New York Times* round-up of the "Best Poetry Books of 2015," David Orr noted that the "poetry books published in a given calendar year usually take up about 18 cubic feet of space, and would thus fit comfortably into the average refrigerator." "Comfortably"? I'm not in a rush to do the math and figure out how many slim volumes fit into a cubic foot—and I suspect Orr isn't taking into account fugitive small press publications or British, Irish, Canadian and other Anglophone books, not to mention the scores of poetry chapbooks, both in print and electronic—but those annually piling-up refrigerators full of books strike my mind's eye as a vast sea, nay, an *ocean* of poems, all of which want to be read and discussed, each one of which has the potential to enthrall me, to excite me, to change my life.

My feeling in the face of all this plethora of poetry to be read, to be considered, to be somehow assessed, reminds me of what Immanuel Kant describes in the *Critique of Judgment* as the "mathematical sublime." Eighteenth-century thinkers made much of the aesthetic category of the "sublime": that which inspires awe, wonderment, the fear of annihilation—as opposed to the merely "beautiful," or aesthetically pleasing. Kant's mathematical sublime is a "sense of the sublime," in Neil Hertz's felicitous summary, "arising out of sheer cognitive exhaustion, the mind blocked not by the threat of overwhelming force, but by the fear of losing count or of being reduced to nothing but counting—this and this and this—with no hope of bringing a long series or a vast scattering under some sort of conceptual unity." My own mind, when I pause to contemplate the vast tracts of contemporary poetry I want to read—or even the substantial lengths of my own "unread poetry" bookshelves—similarly finds itself balked, baffled, thwarted, blocked: and even more so when I cast my attention back over the previous decades and centuries of poetry, and reflect on how little of it I've even glanced at, much less carefully absorbed.

I haven't always had this sense of blockage, bafflement, or inadequacy in the face of the world of poetry. It's a state or place I've arrived at more or less gradually, as I've grown into middle age—or more accurately, as I've grown up. The older I get, the less I know—or the more I realize there is to know that I *don't* know. When I was young I honestly believed that one person could know most everything worth knowing about poetry, and that if I worked hard enough I could be that person. Growing up has meant learning that my own endowments are entirely inadequate to such an ambition. And learning—somewhat comfortingly—that the ambition itself is impossible.

These hard lessons—and I suspect they're only hard for me, that there are lots of readers who at this point are shaking their heads and murmuring, *what a foolish kid! didn't he know from the beginning that the range of poetry surpasses anything any single person can grasp, and that that's one of the wonders and beauties of the whole thing?*—make me suspicious, as I trundle through middle age, of those who make totalizing pronouncements about "what matters" in poetry. Not just the old-school canon- and anthology-makers like Harold Bloom and Helen Vendler, but even those critics and scholars (many of whom, like Brian Reed and Robert Archambeau, I'm much in sympathy with) who are much more modestly trying to chart the direction of the contemporary "scene." I recognize that the effort's absolutely necessary, but at the same time it feels—sub specie aeternitatis—wholly provisional, perhaps futile. Who's to say whether, a hundred years hence, today's essay on conceptual poetry or Flarf won't look as quaint as some Victorian critic's thoughtful assessment of the Spasmodic Poets?

But all the continents of poetry are out there, and each of us makes our own little or big, sketchy or detailed maps to help us navigate. What I know about contemporary poetry I learned mostly outside of the conventional academic maps. I confess I found little to excite me in the few contemporary poets who made it onto the syllabi of my college and grad school courses, nor was I much compelled by most of what my teachers and would-be (institutional) poetic mentors suggested I ought to read. (I'm admitting to a contrarian streak here.) Instead, I pursued a rhizomatic and entirely unsystematic series of routes in my attempt to make some sense of twentieth-century verse.

I read poets, and when those poets wrote about other poets, I would read the latter too. When a contemporary poet wrote an essay or homage to an older poet I already knew, I'd take a look at the contemporary's poetry, as well. Pound and Williams led me to Olson, Zukofsky, Levertov, Creeley. From Zukofsky I went to Oppen, Niedecker, Charles Reznikoff, from them to Michael Heller, Rachel Blau DuPlessis, Norman Finkelstein. Guy Davenport's essays sent me to Jonathan Williams, Ronald Johnson, Ian Hamilton Finlay. Gertrude Stein was on the syllabus at Cornell (*mirabile dictu!*), but I had to find Laura (Riding) Jackson and Mina Loy on my own, from stray remarks in other poets' letters and essays.

Living poets told me who to read, and they were often right. Cecil Giscombe and John Taggart told me to read Nathaniel Mackey, and John urged on me the work of his brilliant former student Pam Rehm. The Language Poet Ted Pearson, in exile in Ithaca, showed me the work of his contemporaries Craig Watson and Phillip Foss, and told me about poets of my own generation I ought to look into—Benjamin Friedlander, Andrew Levy, Melanie Nielson, Jessica Grim, Juliana Spahr, Jennifer Moxley. Robert Morgan brought Geoffrey Hill and John Matthias to campus.

Later, when I'd finished school and was living in the DC area, I fell into the fringes of a lively poetry scene that included Mark Wallace, Tina Darragh, Phyllis Rosenzweig, Tom Mandel, P. Inman, Buck Downs, and Joe Ross, and I met a steady stream of poets who were reading in the various series organized by the indefatigable Rod Smith: Tom Raworth, Jean Day, Leslie Scalapino, Bob Perelman, and many others.

And then of course was there was the simple serendipity of the random bookshop find, the coffee-stained (and inscribed!) copy of Clark Coolidge's *The Maintains* on the dollar rack of Blue Fox Books, or the volumes from Baxter Hathaway's extraordinary Ithaca House Press (which published first books by Perelman, Ray DiPalma, David Melnick, and "Ronald" Silliman) that turned up in every used bookstore in Ithaca.

Over the years, through such reading, through word of mouth, through picking up magazines and books that looked of interest and following through on the names of their authors, editors, and blurbists, I built almost without knowing it a kind of personal canon, a cluster of poets and poetic "tendencies" that compelled me, that stimulated my thinking about poetry and that sparked (if sometimes in opposition) my own writing. I was mapping a few distinct provinces of the great Pangaea of contemporary poetry, and—to invoke a metaphor from Tolkien—if my own map was less like the whole of Middle-earth than the detailed map of the Shire (or as A. R. Ammons might scoff, like that of Mordor), I was most of the time satisfied that it covered most of the stuff I needed to know.

The process has reversed itself over the last couple of decades. I continue to learn about new poets, new periodicals, new poetic "movements" through word of mouth, but the blessed internet has made that word of mouth exponentially more rapid and capacious. I have more poets as "friends" on Facebook than I have ever met (or will ever meet,

THE MATHEMATICAL SUBLIME

I suspect) in the flesh, and they're continually telling me about their new books, the books they're reading, and the poems I ought to read. I can have any book of poetry in print (and many that are out of print) with a few clicks on the Small Press Distribution, Abebooks, or Amazon websites. Vast tracts of things have been digitized and put online, and vast tracts of things are appearing on the web directly, entirely bypassing the whole creaky process of typesetting and print.

And so I find myself in the coils of the mathematical sublime, baulked and dumbfounded by the apparent infinity of invention and creativity that spreads out before me like the Pacific before Keats's "stout Cortez." (Yes, he meant Balboa.) What to read next? What to think about, what to write about next? If I apply my attention to poets A, B, and C, will I be missing the vital, life-changing work of poets X, Y, and Z?

The answer to that last question, of course, is "Yes—for now." Life is short, art long—and wide, and deep. But life allows for second thoughts and recursive turns, and offers the perpetual possibility of new discoveries, both at the farthest reaches of what one imagined (I'm reading Lucan's *Civil War* and Maffeo Vegio's continuation of the *Aeneid*, with very different pleasures) and under one's very nose (there is a long as yet unpublished poem by John Peck on my iPad that I've been working away at: it seems to contain the entire world).

In Kant's account the mathematical sublime has a happy ending, a "compensatory positive movement" (Hertz again): "the mind's exultation in its own rational faculties, in its ability to think a totality that cannot be taken in by the senses." I don't often exult in my own rational faculties (though I'm always pleased when I figure out how to assemble a piece of Ikea furniture), and wrapping my mind around totalities is for me a tough and ephemeral process—I've got it for a moment, and then it's slipped away. Writing about poetry, I realize, is for me less a matter of grasping a totality than it is trying to articulate local pleasures (or displeasures), coming to terms with my experiences of individual poems or books. It's not mapping, but a species of field notes, of local observations. Local observations and field notes can be used to support grander projects, more encompassing attempts to describe landscapes and terrains. But grander projects bespeak grander ambitions. I still cherish a few grand ambitions, and continue to work away (in my own time) at some "big" projects. But I'm content to let the pieces gathered here stand in their own particularity and localness.

* * *

These bits of writing are very much of their moments, called into existence by friends, editors, or Emersonian Whim. I have revised them very little for their collection here—mostly in purging some of the critical jargon to which I occasionally fall prey and in mending references to "forthcoming" volumes which either have failed to appear or which have since the moment of writing come out in rather different forms than I'd anticipated. I've also removed a certain amount of scholarly paraphernalia that might impede the reader-friendliness of a few of the pieces.

Most of these reviews and essays have been previously published (often under different titles, and usually in slightly different forms), and I'm very grateful to the editors who solicited or accepted them. "The Condition of Hebrew" appeared in *Facture: A Journal of Poetry and Poetics*; "A Tinkertoy Poetics" appeared in *The Rumpus*; "Kedging in Time" and "Scars and Fascination" appeared in *Chicago Review*; "The New Colossus, Revisited" appeared in *Studies in American Jewish Literature*; "Passionate, Eccentric Reading" appeared in *Shofar*; "By the Rivers of Babylon" appeared in *Religion and Literature*; "Zuk and Ole Bill" appeared in the *William Carlos Williams Journal*; "A Poetics of Being" appeared in *Big Bridge*; "Resignation and Independence" appeared in the *Notre Dame Review*; "Twilight Gardening" appeared in *Jacket*; "Postmodern Poetry's Blue Period" appeared in *Twentieth-Century Literature*; "Innovation's Explainer" and "The Book of Oz" appeared in *Golden Handcuffs Review*; "Susan Howe's Hauntologies" appeared in *FlashPoint*; "The 'half-fabulous field-ditcher'" appeared in the collection *News from Afar: Ezra Pound and Some Contemporary British Poetries*, edited by Richard Parker; "I am not an occultist" and "The Master of Speech and Speech Itself" appeared in *Talisman: A Journal of Contemporary Poetry and Poetics*.

Writing about poetry, whether sublime or otherwise, has certainly been a long strange trip; but I've had some wonderful companions on the way. When I was an undergraduate, Tom Gardner and the late Allison Sulloway showed me the basics and more—infected me with the virus, as it were. In the (too many) years since, I've talked profitably about poetry with a bunch of people—mentors, colleagues, students, friends—in a variety of venues: in classes, at conferences, before and after readings, over dinner or over drinks, on listservs and in the comments streams of weblogs. The roll call is long (which makes me feel quite blessed), and I'm sure I've forgotten more than a few someones. But thanks to P. Jill Anderson, Robert Archambeau, Ed Baker, Katherine Baluta, Zach Barocas, Charles Bernstein, Daniel Bouchard, Jamie Brown, Sally Connolly, Joshua Corey, Joseph Donahue, Thom Donovan, Steven Fama, Curtis Faville, A. J. Ferguson, Norman Finkelstein, Debra Fried, Benjamin Friedlander, Raymond Gibson, Roger Gilbert, C. S. Giscombe, Alan Golding, Henry Gould, Peggy Hamilton, Michael Heller, Janet Holmes, Lisa Howe, Susan Howe, William Howe, Kent Johnson, David Kaufmann, David Kellogg, David LoSchiavo, Nathaniel Mackey, John Matthias, Vance Maverick, Jonathan Mayhew, Emily Miller Mlcak, Robert Morgan, Paul Naylor, David Need, Aldon Nielsen, T. A. Noonan, Peter O'Leary, Michael J. Pagán, Ted Pearson, Bob Perelman, Marjorie Perloff, Michael Peverett, Patrick Pritchett, Peter Quartermain, Laura Quinlan, Susan M. Schultz, Eric Murphy Selinger, Don Share, Robert Sheppard, Jessica Smith, Sam Stoloff, Jake Syersak, John Taggart, John Tipton, Mark Wallace, Tyrone Williams, and two very smart bloggers I know only as "Sisyphus" and "Undine." As always, the biggest thanks—gratitude beyond words—goes to the home team: Jennifer, Pippa, and Daphne.

1. REVIEWS

The Condition of Hebrew

Geoffrey Hill, *Speech! Speech!* (Counterpoint, 2000)

Geoffrey Hill made a name for himself as the most single most impressive poet of the school of Eliot and Empson, the heir of Eliot's relentless allusiveness and Empson's late-metaphysical ambiguity. His verse was formally traditional, formidably erudite, and remarkably dense. In a series of collections published from the late 1950s to the mid-1980s, he played variation after agonized variation on a limited number of themes: the burdens of history's atrocities, from the Wars of the Roses to the Holocaust; the plight of the religiously-inclined poet in a world from which God seemed to have fled, or toward which God seemed to manifest only a malevolent face; and the paradox of the artist's task, making objects of aesthetic contemplation out of the unspeakably sordid materials of human history. Along the way he became a Cambridge don and published two volumes of criticism (*The Lords of Limit* and *The Enemy's Country*) that rivaled Louis Zukofsky in the density of their prose and the palpable seriousness of their thought. This was heavy stuff indeed, and by the end of the eighties Hill was acclaimed by many in the mainstream poetry establishment—Donald Hall, Harold Bloom, John Hollander—as the most important English poet of our day.

Such claims, of course, buttered few parsnips for the partisans of Hill's colleague across the quad, that other Cambridge don J.H. Prynne. That isn't to say that Hill was an irredeemable traditionalist—his 1971 *Mercian Hymns*, a series of prose poems that crosscut the social criticism of John Ruskin, the chronicled history of medieval England, and the working-class *Bildungsromane* so popular in 1960s Britain into a haunting, timeless series of snapshots, showed that he was by no means constrained to the sonnets and iambic pentameter his other poems favored. But for the followers of the "New American Poetry" of the 1960s and its various offshoots, and for their British counterparts, the readers of Prynne, Tom Raworth, and Andrew Crozier, Hill represented the same Tradition that had thrown up

Philip Larkin as the voice of postwar England. Hill, no matter how he might tinker with the forms of his verse, spoke for the establishment. Perhaps with *Speech! Speech!* all that will change.

The simplest way of putting this is that Hill's work has undergone a sea change, that the man's poetry, while still recognizably his own, has become altogether something new. Put it down to change of scenery, perhaps (since 1988 Hill has taught at Boston University); put it down to a happy marriage (to Alice Goodman, the librettist for John Adams's operas *Nixon in China* and *The Death of Klinghoffer*); or put it down, uncharitably, to medication. In a recent *Paris Review* interview, Hill revealed that much of his newfound personal happiness is the result of finally finding a successful treatment for what amounted to a lifelong "chronic depression, which was accompanied by various exhausting obsessive-compulsive phobias." I'm not just repeating personal tidbits here; it's in *Speech! Speech!*:

> How is it tuned, how can it be un-
> tuned, with lithium, this harp of nerves? Fare well
> my daimon, inconstant
> measures, mood- and mind-stress, heart's rhythm
> suspensive.

Frankly, I'm not much interested in the chemical sources of Hill's poetic in *Speech! Speech!* (God only knows how much of the fragmentation and experimentation of the New American Poetry was pharmaceutically fueled—and again, who cares?) But I'm terrifically moved by the new territory into which his poetry has pushed.

The ground was prepared in 1998's *The Triumph of Love*, a 150-section long poem that revisited Hill's childhood and that brooded over the horrific history of twentieth-century Europe. Not new themes for Hill, but what was new was the flexible free verse of the poetry, the pervasive sense of bitter humor, and a newfound heteroglossia, the irruption of other's voices—commentators, copyeditors, naysayers, errata sheets—into the previously unruffled texture of the verse. "Rancorous, narcissistic old sod," one voice says, "what / makes him go on?" A list of errata intrudes:

> For wordly, read worldly; for in equity, inequity;
> for religious read religiose; for distinction
> detestation. Take accessible to mean
> acceptable, accommodating, openly servile.
> *Is that right, Missis, or is that right?* I don't
> care what I say, do I?

There is a newly sardonic tone to the poetry of *Triumph of Love*, a jaunty punchiness that both acknowledges that Hill's obsessions might have grown stale for his readers and castigates those readers for their callow and callous lack of patience. "I / write for the dead, *N.*, *N.*, [two unnamed Nobel laureates] for the living"—line break—"dead."

There had always been an strong element of self-consciousness in Hill's broodings over those whom history has maimed and eliminated. This was a poet for whom the poetry of witness was no light matter, no fashionable mode to be donned or doffed: one who did not live through the Holocaust—as Hill himself, born in Worcestershire in 1932, did not—might still bear witness to that black time, but it was a witness that had to be at all points qualified and questioned, lest the poet's urge for making begin, in a process itself obscene, to find history's obscenities mere *materia poetica*. Midway through "September Song" (from *King Log*, 1968), a poem memorializing an unnamed child murdered by the Nazis, Hill writes, "(I have made / an elegy for myself it / is true)." An elegy for himself—for this child is almost precisely Hill's own age, and the poet has written with that heavy coincidence much on his mind; and an elegy for himself, for what poet writes but on some level to please that harshest of critics, her- or himself? Such self-consciousness and seriousness of purpose were everywhere evident in *The Triumph of Love*, but here his doubts and second thoughts had been externalized, given voice by a bevy of carping critics—"Croker, MacSikker, O'Shem"—and continually undercut both by the poet's own voice and by the bracketed interjections of some bean-counting textual critic and commentator: when Hill writes "I am not too far from the end," this voice interjects, "[of the sequence—ed]." In the end, however, *The Triumph of Love* describes the poem in terms that could fit all of Hill's work to date; it is "*a sad and angry consolation.*"

While the sadness is not so evident in *Speech! Speech!*, the anger is here in God's plenty, and it most often takes the form of Swift's satirical "savage indignation." This is nothing if not a savage piece of writing. The poem is in 120 twelve-line (but unrhymed) sections, one for each of the Marquis de Sade's days of Sodom; and the City of the Plain, if we are to follow Hill's implied analogy, is our own media-saturated culture. Hill once described his stolid "Funeral Music," a sequence revolving around the Wars of the Roses, as "a florid grim music broken by grunts and shrieks." A renaissance masque, perhaps, performed by the inmates of Weiss's *Marat/Sade*. *Speech! Speech!*'s music is of a more modern variety, the florid samples, quotes, and interjections of hip-hop. "Hopefully, RAPMASTER," Hill writes, "I can take stock / how best to oút-ráp you. Like Herod / raging in the street-pageants | work the crowd" (47). The poem is sprinkled with these accents and virgules, even as the voice we recognize as Hill's is interrupted by incessant and semi-random irruptions of mediaspeak. It is as if Gerard Manly Hopkins (painfully earnest about those pedantic accents, on which the proper meaning of his verses depended) had been rewritten by Bruce Andrews:

> *Credo* (car radio) | even as I muse
> through tactics, passive aggressions, wound-up
> laughter from the claques. HAS BEEN | EDITED.
> NOT CLEARED FOR PUBLICATION. Don't bleep shop.
> Accept contingencies. Honour

the *duende*. Revoke a late
vocation to silence. THÁT'S ALL RÍGHT THEN.

Hill's essays had been models of deeply-thought-through, painstakingly developed argument; is such thought, such argument any longer possible in a culture broken into sound-bites, pursuing its own tail through the labyrinths of the world-wide web?

       Why and how
  in these orations do I twist my text?
APPLY FOR FAST RELIEF. Dystopia
on Internet: profiles of the new age;
great gifts unprized; craven audacity's
shockers; glow-in-the-dark geriatric
wigs from old candy-floss (*cat-calls, cheers*).
Starved fourteenth-century mystics write of LOVE.
When in doubt perform. Stick to the much-used
CHECKMATE condom (*laughter, cries of 'shame'*).

Audience response, as in the passage above, is much in evidence in this poem, whose title plays upon its cover art, a lithograph by Daumier depicting a hall full of ill-favored Parisian bourgeoisie, top hats upon their knees, transfixed with laughter and applause: "*On dit que les Parisiens sont difficiles à satisfaire*"—they say Parisians are hard to please. Obviously not. Throughout these sections, Hill castigates not merely himself but his audience as well; and the indictment is not only of the readers of poetry who remain satisfied with the tracings of middle-class angst churned out by the mainstream poetic culture of both Britain and America—it extends to British and American culture as a whole. We have forgotten, in a flurry of headlines, thirty-second news stories, graphic-heavy webpages, and advertising images, everything important about the world in which we live, the culture we have inherited. Where is history, where is responsibility? The Roman

Catholic pilgrimage tradition (always attractive to Hill, though never embraced) finds its contemporary analogue in the high-tech media circus that is Princess Diana's memorial service:

> Where áre we? Lourdes? SOME sodding mystery tour.
> Whát do you meán | a break? Pisses me off.
> Great singer Elton John though. CHRIST
> ALMIGHTY—even the buses are kneeling!

Have we reached the point where we need "Footnotes / to explain BIRKENAU, BUCHENWALD, BURNHAM BEECHES, DUMBARTON OAKS, HOLLYWOOD"?

Hill bites at his readers, and I suspect some of his readers will bite back. (Savage reviews of *Speech! Speech!* have already begun trickling in from the bulwarks of conservative verse culture.) And while one might muse skeptically upon the avant-garde conversion experience of Jorie Graham, Hill has by no means become a Language poet in his old age: there is still a locatable central voice to *Speech! Speech!*, a voice recognizable as Hill's own. That voice is sad, bitter, sardonic, and immensely learned. ("Assume the earphones. Not / music. Hebrew. Poetry aspires / to the condition of Hebrew.") Through the fog and static of contemporary culture, it calls out in the tones of the writer I've decided is Hill's tutelary spirit—the Victorian art historian and social critic John Ruskin. Ruskin took it upon himself, with immense eloquence and rage, to be the conscience of his age, and some would say that self-assumed responsibility drove him mad. Let me rephrase my earlier formulation, then: rather than Hopkins rewritten by Bruce Andrews, *Speech! Speech!* is an agon between John Ruskin and the Internet, Ruskin and the remote control. It is an immensely funny but painfully moving poem, more often than not at the same time. *The Triumph of Love* ended with a return to Hill's boyhood Romsley, "a sad and bitter consolation." *Speech! Speech!* ends with a *Waste Land*-like jumble of phrases from the headlines, the classics, and the psalter, and offers little consolation to the reader adrift—like the poet—in a world of corporate phrase:

> O TIME-LIFE, dó
> try to be reasonable; you háve the power.
> At least pass me the oxygen. Too late.
> AMOR. MAN IN A COMA, MA'AM. NEMO. AMEN.

A Tinkertoy Poetics

Charles Bernstein, *All the Whiskey in Heaven: Selected Poems* (Farrar, Straus and Giroux, 2010)

One may debate the ultimate morality of western capitalism, but one can't deny its ingenuity. I'm repeatedly impressed by how the market can manufacture a thousand different varieties of an item—toothbrushes, carbonated beverages, bedspreads, pop songs—and then ferret out the consumers whose taste matches each obscure product. (Me, I'm a Peach Nehi guy.) And in the great literary Mall of America, there're a whole lot of different flavors of poet on sale these days: the plainspoken but witty; the achingly vulnerable and painfully oblique; the thoughtful and earnest, working with furrowed brow to get across *what you ought to know*; the angrily political (almost always from the Left, since Republicans figured out a long time ago that poetry doesn't pay); the nimble-tongued, virtuosic rapper-slammers; and so forth.

I think of Charles Bernstein as a Tinkertoy poet. You remember those masses of rods and wheels and whatchamacallits that you spent hours putting together in various Rube Goldberg-like imitations of a car or a steam shovel or a skyscraper? That's pretty much how Bernstein approaches language in a lot of his work, except that he's not interested in making the snazzy racecar or the dumptruck pictured on the Tinkertoy box; he'd rather find out what sort of cool, interesting, weird combinations he can come up with by sticking words, phrases, even letters together at random, or by deliberately frustrating all of what we think of as the "normal" poet's impulses—you know, the desire to "express" oneself, to make something "beautiful," to "say something."

Bernstein's Tinkertoy experimentalism will make *All the Whiskey in Heaven*, a comprehensive selection of some three decades of his poetry, rather heavy going for many readers. Bernstein has spent much of his career being published by tiny hole-in-the-wall presses, and I wondered if this collection, his first with a major trade press, was going to downplay his more hard-nosedly weird work. But I needn't have worried. Yes, here we have "Lift Off," a two-page poem transcribed from a typewriter correction ribbon ("HH/ ie,s obVrsxr;atjrn dugh seineopcv i iibalfmgmMw"), "Asylum," whose words and phrases are all collaged from Erving Goffman's *Asylums: Essays on the Social Situation of Mental Patients and Other Inmates*, and "A Defence of Poetry," something of a poetics essay in the form of a letter typed at white-hot speed in the old pre-autocorrect days, reckless typos and all:

> My problem with deploying a term liek
> nonelen
> in these cases is acutually similar to
> your
> cirtique of the term ideopigical
> unamlsing as a too-broad unanuajce
> interprestive proacdeure.

Some readers will find such hijinks amusing but ephemeral; others (who'll have little more patience for Bernstein's marginally less radical modes of juxtaposing unrelated words, phrases, and sentences) will take them as an assault on the idea of poetry itself, at least as it's been represented in mainstream American culture over the last couple of centuries. I think it's safe to say that Bernstein would subscribe to that last description. His poems are to the conventional "well-formed" personal poem what Henny Youngman's one-liners ("Take my wife—please!") were to the anecdotal jokes of the 1930s, or what Andy Kaufman's conceptual art ("T'ank you veddy much") was to standup comedy of the 1970s.

In short, Bernstein is taking apart the structures of conventional poetry, and more generally of the language we use every day—and which in turn uses us—in order to return us to a more basic relationship with language itself, and with the social relations which language encodes and enforces. "Foreign Body Sensation," for instance, cobbling together sentences from a variety of disparate résumés and self-descriptions, shows how the language of American can-do-ness melts the vocational, spiritual, artistic, and political into a single optimistic sludge:

> I am especially interested in the treatment of depression. With my Lord and Savior Jesus Christ at the center of my life, I have found real Joy and Purpose in dedicating myself to the Truth of His Teaching as Written in the Bible. What gives the job its excitement is working with Stan Richards, a nationally recognized creative wizard: *Adweek* recently named our agency among the eight most creative in the U. S.

Bernstein is maybe the best-known of the "Language Poets," a loose coalition of left-leaning avant-gardists who emerged in the 1970s and 1980s. The Language Poets combined a fearsome experimentalism (they read Gertrude Stein and Louis Zukofsky, not Wallace Stevens or Robert Lowell) with an implacable intellectualism (their essays and manifestos—lots of them—showed a disturbing familiarity with French and Russian cultural theory) and a snarling disdain for "mainstream" literary culture (the *New Yorker*, the MFA industry). It's no wonder they were once regarded with fear and loathing in creative writing programs across the country.

Bernstein has the advantage over many of his fellow Language Poets of being pretty consistently funny. One of the best bits of the late 1990s series of Yellow Pages TV ads featuring Jon Lovitz as "The Man Who Wrote the Yellow Pages" was an interview with Bernstein as "The Critic," who compared the Yellow Pages to Homer, Dante, and Pound ("a poem including history"), and leafed through a half-dozen pages beginning "Fence,"—"Amazing, that repetition of *Fence*!" I get the feeling he was improvising there, at once dead serious and aware of the ludicrousness of the moment—like the best comics.

I quoted Henny Youngman earlier, and Youngman is clearly one of Bernstein's tutelary deities (as he puts it in "Of Time and the Line,"

George Burns "weaves lines together by means of a picaresque narrative; / not so Henny Youngman, whose lines are strictly paratactic"). Sure, Bernstein's a Marxist, but the Marx in question is as much Groucho, Chico, or Harpo as it is Karl. "Dear Mr. Fanelli" is a bravura piece of passive-aggressive standup, a long letter addressed to a New York subway administrator whose picture in the station invites comments from transit passengers:

> Mr.
> Fanelli—there are
> a lot of people sleeping
> in the 79th street station
> and it makes me sad
> to think they have no
> home to go to. Mr.
> Fanelli, do you think
> you could find a more
> comfortable place for them
> to rest? It's pretty noisy
> in the subway ...

Much of Bernstein's humor falls in the category of the sophisticated literary in-joke, but in recent years he's taken up a broader and rather more savage brush, attacking the more retrograde tendencies in American culture in a kind of mock-incompetent doggerel:

> Daddy loves me this I know
> Cause my granddad told me so
> Though he beats me blue and black
> That's because I'm full of crap ("The Boy Soprano")

Bernstein's earlier work is among the most audaciously exploratory language-shaping I know. Lately, however, he's been exploring the emotional potential of the oldest and most basic forms of meter and rhyme, the musical simplicities of the ballad tradition. In "Rivulets of the Dead Jew" he achieves a childlike, Seussian simplicity while touching the emotional mystery of the oldest ballads:

> I've got a date with a
> Bumble bee, bumble bee
> I've got a date with a
> wee bonnie wee
> and ahurtling we will go

Bernstein's latest works—in particular his admonition to his son, "The Ballad of the Girly Man," and the collection's title poem, "All the Whiskey in Heaven"—attempt to discover a real emotional immediacy in an idiom so bare, so mawkishly awkward, that they border on real doggerel. What's most wonderful is that they succeed, giving us a kind of double vision of real passion shining through deliberately awful verse, like the brilliance and pathos, the simultaneous amateurishness and heroic aspiration that the closest watchers could read in Andy Kaufman's lip-synced version of the "Mighty Mouse" song.

Kedging in Time

John Matthias, *Kedging: New Poems* (Salt Publishing, 2007)

John Matthias's big *New Selected Poems* of 2004 had an unfortunate air of closure, ending as it did with the wistful "Swell," a poem every bit as redolent of mortality as E. B. White's oddly parallel essay "Once More to the Lake." The hushed finality of "Swell" made melancholy reading, particularly in light of the vein of high-tech, sometimes zany late modernism Matthias had begun to mine in his previous book, *Working Progress, Working Title* (2002). The melancholy and sense of mortality are still in evidence in *Kedging: New Poems*— sometimes overwhelmingly so—but this new collection, in particular the sequence "The Memoirists" and the two long poems "Laundry Lists and Manifestoes" and "Kedging in Time," makes it abundantly clear that Matthias, though never an immensely prolific poet, is by no means shutting up shop, but has entered a period of renewed invention and rather high-spirited exploration.

Matthias, as has often been noted, is one of a group of poets (others include Robert Hass, Robert Pinsky, James McMichael, and John Peck) who studied at Stanford under that crusty arch-formalist and anti-modernist Yvor Winters. Winters's tutelage seems to have had unexpected consequences in at least two cases, for Peck and Matthias have proved themselves more or less intransigently wedded to high modernist modes of juxtaposition and literary and historical allusion, in the process falling between the stools of laureateship-ready apprehensibility (Hass and Pinsky) and "postmodernist" textuality (the Language Poets). Peck's language is an astonishingly taut and intricately wrought weave which incorporates both complex formal and metrical patterns and flights of "poetic" diction that would make most workshop leaders blush. Matthias, in contrast, tends toward a midwestern flatness, a plainspoken idiom that only occasionally rises to lyrical heights, and which is liable to achieve its most impressive effects through patient accrual rather than vatic leaps.

The first section of *Kedging*, "Post-Anecdotal," consists of short poems in a—well—anecdotal mode. There are a number of elegies, farewells to Matthias's friends and fellow-workers in the field of letters, including the translator Anthony Kerrigan and the polymathic Guy Davenport. There are many personal poems here, memories of childhood and of youthful brushes with the great, and there are some definite notes of sadness: "Missing Cynouai" and "For My Last Reader" (the latter leavened with wryness). There is also some hilarity: the delicious shaggy-dog tale of "Junior Brawner," and the pitch-perfect parody of recent Geoffrey Hill in the second section of "Hoosier Horloge."

The middle section of the book, "The Cotranslator's Dilemma," presents twenty or so pages of the Swedish poets on whose English versions Matthias has collaborated: Jesper Svenbro, Göran Printz-Påhlson, Tomas Tranströmer, and Göran Sonnevi. All of these poems have previously appeared in book form, but one is glad to see them again, especially the poems of Svenbro, a renowned classicist whose poetry performs a dazzling mediation between twentieth-century Scandinavia and the classical Mediterranean. (*Three-Toed Gull*, a full collection of Matthias's versions of Svenbro, was published by Northwestern University Press in 2003: it is a very rich book indeed.)

The heart of *Kedging*, however lies in the book's three long projects. "The Memoirists" is the most straightforward of these, a sequence of five poems based on the lives and writings of five celebrated memoirists: Lorenzo Da Ponte, the librettist of Mozart's Italian operas, who later emigrated to the United States where he was among other things a grocer in Philadelphia; Edward John Trelawney, the friend and biographer of Shelley and Byron, whose own autobiography is a tissue of fantasy-projections of a piratical youth; Frederick Rolfe, Baron Corvo, the fin-de-siècle eccentric whose life and self-mystifications fuel A. J. A. Symons's *The Quest for Corvo*; Céleste Albaret, Marcel Proust's devoted housekeeper; and the songwriter Vernon Duke, born Vladimir Dukelsky, whose career moved between the "high" art of Diaghilev and Prokofiev and Tin Pan Alley. Each memoirist's life story is recounted in quotation and narrative fragments formed into eight-line stanzas, and each separate poem is cunningly joined to its neighbors through thematic or lexical repetition. Like Davenport in his stories and essays, Matthias has a clear relish for the glimmering detail, the anecdote that encapsulates his subject's sensibility. Indeed, I would hazard, Matthias is the closest thing we have to a Davenport in verse.

The title poem, "Kedging in Time," is a rather more ambitious affair. Over some twenty-five pages, Matthias constructs a palimpsest of late-imperial British naval history from before the Great War, through the debacle of Gallipoli, to the day of the surrender of the Kaiser's fleet, *der Tag*. This history is refracted through the sensibility and family connections of Pamela Adams, the daughter and wife of British Navy captains (and Matthias's mother-in-law), and is punctuated and salted with references to various popular fictions of the early twentieth century: Erskine Childers's *The Riddle of the Sands*, Anthony Hope's *The Prisoner of Zenda*, and John Buchan's *Greenmantle* and *The Thirty-Nine Steps* (as well as Hitchcock's film adaptation of that novel). Matthias cannily avoids condescension in name-dropping these classics of the "boys' own" genre; indeed, he's able to evoke a sense of what tremendous reads these oft-neglected volumes are, much as he did with Robert Louis Stevenson's *Kidnapped* and Sir Walter Scott's *Waverley* in "Northern Summer," an earlier long poem.

To "kedge," an epigraph to the poem explains, is "To warp a ship, or move it from one position to another by winding in a hawser attached to a small anchor dropped at some distance." In the genial and roundabout essay "Kedging in *Kedging in Time*," included as part of *Kedging*'s sixth section, "The Back of the Book," Matthias describes his use of these prior texts (along with various memoirs, histories, and logbooks): they are "secure holds for the kedge-anchor of my reefed verbal craft." This is a bit too diffident, I fear; it gives the impression of the poem as an unwieldy, engineless hulk being dragged from one extratextual anchor-point to the next. For this reader, "Kedging in Time" seems similar in mode to any number of Matthias's earlier long poems: a resonant structure of historical, literary, and personal particulars held in uneasy tension, traversed by the poet's own restless, connection-seeking sensibility. And "Kedging in Time" is particularly colored with the bittersweet aura of familial associations, touched with the melancholy sense that the poem is in some way a leave-taking of the Britain that has furnished the material for so much of Matthias's earlier work.

Far more sprightly is *Kedging*'s other long project, "Laundry Lists and Manifestoes." This twenty-two section poem takes its title from a couple of sentences of A. S. Byatt's, quoted among its epigraphs: "People often leave no record of the most critical or passionate moments of their lives. They leave laundry lists and manifestoes." The biographer and archival researcher know how true this is, how often the emotional center of a subject's life can only be inferred or, worse, speculated upon: the paper trails of even the most famous often consist only of the more rarefied, strategic public pronouncements—"manifestoes"—and the most mundane quotidian records—"laundry lists." But, as Matthias quotes Auden, "never trust a critic who does not like lists / The genealogies in Genesis, the Catalogue of Ships": and what a delightful romp Matthias manages to conjure out of such arrays!

The poem begins with two ur-laundry-scenes: Nausicaa, the Phaeacian princess who encounters the shipwrecked Odysseus while doing the royal family's wash, and Japheth's wife—unnamed, as so many women in the Hebrew Bible—preparing to do a major clean-up after the Flood (which has lasted well over half a year). The dovetailing of events is typically Matthian. Ham's witnessing of his father Noah's drunken nakedness leads directly to Odysseus's concealing of his genitals with "Just a leafy twig," but both events are narrated with a lubricious jauntiness quite unlike their ancient originals: "She asked to see his manifest. Alas, he said, I've lost it with / My ship and all my men, but you can put this on / Your laundry list—and took away the twig."

A "manifest," of course, is a type of list (as well as being related to "manifesto"), and Matthias's poem derives much of its delicious momentum from playing the scales of such puns and etymological relations: *list* becomes *manifest, catalogue, account,* all of them proliferating into their related terms—*manifesto, manifestation, accounting.* Nausicaa's laundry includes "her thong, her super-low-cut jeans, her black lace / Demi-bra and other things she'd ordered from the *catalogue.*" And *list* becomes *list* (verb, as in Hamlet's father's "List, list, O, list!"), *listener, listless,* and so forth. The poem veers through a forest of lists and catalogues—"genealogies in Genesis, the Catalogue of Ships," Don Giovanni's lovers, famous poems whose first lines begin with "M," items Robinson Crusoe has managed to salvage from his shipwreck—sparking them off of various manifestoes, in particular the aggressive pronouncements of various modernist movements, from Marinetti's (Italian) Futurism to Khlebnikov's (Russian) Futurism and Malevich's Suprematism. Toward the end, "Laundry Lists and Manifestoes" becomes a meditation on creativity, communication, and technology, from the evolution of the human hand to Donna Haraway's cyborg theory.

I suspect that Matthias regards the high-spirited romp of "Laundry Lists and Manifestoes" as somewhat less *serious*, less ballasted with *gravitas*, than the nostalgically historical "Kedging in Time." But it's a lovely thing that he can pull off two such divergent projects in a single volume, and with such assurance and élan. Matthias the wry melancholic may gloom over the prospect of "My Last Reader" replacing his book "On the shelf, where it continues—/ *Comerado, this was a man!*—/ Moldering and moldering to dust," but Matthias the poet continues to produce works of delightful freshness and refreshing ambition.

THE NEW COLOSSUS, REVISITED

Jonathan N. Barron and Eric Murphy Selinger, eds., *Jewish American Poetry: Poems, Commentary, and Reflections* (Brandeis University Press, 2000)

Jonathan N. Barron and Eric Murphy Selinger begin their collection *Jewish American Poetry* with a text that's familiar even to readers who have no specific knowledge of the poetry written by American Jews. "Give me your tired, your poor, / Your huddled masses yearning to breathe free," and so forth—the last five lines of Emma Lazarus's sonnet "The New Colossus"—may not be poetry of a high order, but a happy twist of history has inscribed them on the base of perhaps the most universally recognized emblem of America's relationship with world Jewry: the Statue of Liberty. And here they are again, at last reunited with the poem's other nine and a half lines, kicking off a collection of "poems, commentary, and reflections" by contemporary American Jewish poets and scholars of that poetry.

Lazarus herself was no immigrant, and her family—one parent Ashkenazi, the other Sephardic—could trace their American roots back to the Revolution. Her own awakening to matters Jewish came only in her early thirties, when she read George Eliot's *Daniel Deronda*, and when she learned of the vicious pogroms following Czar Alexander II's assassination in 1881. Ralph Waldo Emerson himself, the grand old man of American letters, called Lazarus "the great Hebrew poetess." (Not as fine a compliment as that which he addressed to Whitman in 1855—"I greet you at the beginning of a great career"—but as Adam Sandler would say, "not too shabby," either.) He seemed to have second thoughts, however, and Lazarus did not appear in *Parnassus*, his anthology of his favorite American poems. She was understandably miffed, though her shade ought to take comfort in the fact that neither Whitman, Poe nor Dickinson was included, either. "By way of recompense," then, both for Emerson's editorial faux pas and for the exigencies of space faced by civic stonecutters, Barron and Selinger have given "The New Colossus" pride of place in their new, almost dazzlingly broad compilation.

There's a feeling of seeking recompense throughout the editorial material here. It's not, of course, that Jewish American writing in general hasn't received its share of attention—after all, two of America's Nobel laureates, Isaac Bashevis Singer and Saul Bellow, have been Jews, and articles and books by the score continue to be written on the holy trinity of Bellow, Roth, and Malamud. It's just that Jewish American *poetry* seems to have gotten the short end of the institutional stick. Barron and Selinger's collection is itself a sign that this is changing, along with Steven J. Rubin's anthology *Telling and Remembering: A Century of American Jewish Poetry* and a number of recent scholarly monographs.

Rubin's anthology is wonderfully broad and inclusive, but the attention paid to Jewish American poetry in these recent critical books tends to focus on handfuls of poets, rather than the entire heterogeneous scene. Barron and Selinger aim to put this right. Here's an anthology that includes both Language Poets and New Formalists (or, as some of them prefer, "Expansive Poets"—whatever that means), both feminists and ethnopoets, both performance poets and academic chairholders. *Jewish American Poetry* is by no means perfect or entirely satisfying, but it's a splendid, fascinating, and important book. Could I put it down? Well, a number of pieces here sorely tempted me to do just that, but there was always something coming up that rewarded persistence.

Barron and Selinger have come up with a elegant structure for this collection. The first part of the book, "Poems and Commentary," presents a single poem by each of twenty-six poets, followed by a prose commentary by the poet. The second part, "Reflections," presents nine essays addressing a wide range of topics concerning Jewish American poetry. A couple of the essayists are poets to boot, and use their own poetry as grist for the critical mill; it makes for a wonderful bleed-through between the various sections of the collection. Indeed, it's clear that Barron and Selinger are addressing *Jewish American Poetry* to a more general audience than the typical university press book might reach—at the very least an audience that isn't strictly literary. (The book's included in Brandeis's series in "American Jewish History, Culture, and Life"—like it says in the storefront of the Judaica shop down the street, "If it's Jewish, we've got it!")

In practice, that means that Barron and Selinger begin their introduction with a comprehensive history of American poetry—in all of eleven pages. To call this overview "potted" would perhaps be too kind. Barron and Selinger do their darnedest to cram everybody in, but there's still plenty of omissions to kvetch about, and plenty of strange bedfellows. Robert Frost would no doubt be shifting in his dour pentameter grave to find himself a "modernist" along with Stein, Williams, and Pound, while the editors dub Muriel Rukeyser (born 1913) the "third great Jewish American poet" (Lazarus is the first, Gertrude Stein number two) even as they discuss Louis Zukofsky (born 1904) in the same section. Supporting arguments, please?

But I'm not sure I've ever met an introduction I entirely liked, and the real meat of *Jewish American Poetry* lies in the poems and commentaries. There is true richness and an impressive inclusiveness here. I'll be very upfront about this: I'm really ambivalent about the whole genre of the poets commenting on their own work. Way too many poetry readings have been ruined for me by readers who insist on prefacing their poems with inane and pedestrian commentary, as if their listeners were unable to follow anything more complex than a *People* magazine lead article. Some of these poem-commentary pairings have a bit of the feel of one of those readings ("This next poem I wrote when I was twenty-three years old and living in Paris…"), but what makes all the difference is the particular direction in which Barron and Selinger have slanted the commentaries. "Don't just tell us about the poem," I can imagine them saying, "tell us what makes the poem *Jewish*."

Some poets respond directly. Charles Bernstein, after a longish list poem in which he runs through a gamut of subject-positions ("I am a capitalist poet in Leningrad / and a socialist poet in St. Petersburg; / a bourgeois poet at Zabar's, a union poet / in Albany..."), muses, "But is it Jewish? / –I think, probably, maybe so / But it could also be not Jewish / –Exactly." The performance poet Hal Sirowitz, commenting on his painfully funny (funnily painful?) "Sons," notes baldly, "the poem is about having to exist outside the dominant religion. Being Jewish made me feel like an outsider." Maxine Kumin uses her commentary space after "For Anne at Passover" to get back at some anonymous reviewer of forty years ago who questioned the poem's Jewishness. (I'll take Kumin's word for the "Jewish consciousness" she claims is present in much of her work, but I also think the snide *Philadelphia Enquirer* reader of 1961 was right; let the reader judge.)

Other poets take the opportunity to give us thumbnail sketches of their careers or moments in their careers, using matters Jewish as the pivot around which to recount how they came to poetry and developed therein. Chana Bloch's commentary on her "Don't Tell the Children" is one of these, as is Gerald Stern's memoir of his youth in Paris (commenting on a poem entitled, oddly enough, "Paris"). It's in a collection like this that one can really see the faultlines in American poetry. Stern, like Kumin, Marge Piercy, Alan Shapiro, Philip Levine, and others, is perfectly happy working within the loose free-verse, personal-voice form of the "workshop" aesthetic ubiquitous in contemporary American poetry (and American MFA programs) toward the end of the twentieth century. The obvious way to comment upon such a poem, and to comment upon its Jewish elements, is to talk about how one's own experience has informed it. So we learn about Levine's childhood, Piercy's search for just the right papercut for a book jacket, Shapiro's relationship with his father, and Albert Goldbarth's first minyan ("I didn't *want* to; but I went. I *wanted* to—what? Watch television? Play with my willie?").

Drawing these direct lines between life and art, however, is more problematic for poets who are committed to some version of the poem as *textual* object separate from the poet's experience. John

Hollander phrases his own version elegantly—"poems, unlike pieces of expository prose of any length, don't *have* 'subjects,' but rather are representational objects themselves"—and his explication of his own "At the New Year" is as precise, thoughtful, and coolly distant as any of his readings of Milton or the metaphysical poets. Bob Perelman, like Charles Bernstein usually roped into the Language Poetry camp, doesn't really address his poem "Chaim Soutine" much at all, but muses briefly on his own relation to Judaism; his prose has the same edgy humor as his poetry: "I was not beaten up as a child, either by Jews or for being Jewish.... You say eternal, I say ahistorical...." He's content to let the poem speak for itself, and it does, eloquently.

Happily, most of these twenty-six poets seize their opportunity at commentary gladly, producing mini-essays on poetry and Jewishness, some of which are striking, haunting, and memorable. Allen Grossman's commentary on "How to Do Things with Tears" has the thoughtful, almost portentous seriousness that's always fascinated me in his prose, even while the poem itself doesn't quite click for me. Norman Finkelstein's splendid Talmudic parable, "Acher," is only enriched, deepened, and made more mysterious by his meditation on the sources behind the poem and his speculations about its implications. Jerome Rothenberg's commentary on his intentionally brutal "Noch Aushvits (After Auschwitz)" is almost a full-length essay on Jewishness and poetry from one of Jewish American poetry's most consistently category-bounding practitioners. And while I'm not at all taken with Marcia Falk's "Winter Solstice"—it seems to embody the kind of imagistic simplifications that all too often get poems into the prayerbooks (and for Unitarians, into the hymnals)—her commentary on the poem is a sharp, resonant, and deeply felt exploration of what it means to write lyrics that might be read in a communal, liturgical context.

And then there are some of these doublets that I'm happy to have just for the sake of the poems. Ammiel Alcalay's commentary on the excerpt from *the cairo notebooks* isn't particularly memorable, but the poem itself is a knockout, piecing the political, the historical, and the sensual into a fragmented and resonant mosaic. I like Jacqueline Osherow's commentary on "Scattered Psalms: XI (Dead Men's Praise)," but I'm totally enamored with the poem itself. It's a talky, funny, and profound thinking through of the relationship between Jewishness, death, liturgy, Yiddish poetry, poetry itself, and several other topics, roping in the Yiddish poet Yakov Glatstein, the Psalmist David, Georg Friedrich Handel, and the clumsy American Christian pronunciation of "Hallelujah."

And then there are the failures (though thankfully, rather few). C. K. Williams's gushy, faux-naïve commentary on "The Vessel" is pretty much effaced by the poem's own rampant, undisciplined gush. Eleanor Wilner explicates her "Miriam's Song"—in itself not a subtle poem by any stretch of the imagination—in a hectoring, unsubtly politicized four pages that leave no warmongering phallocracy unstoned. But I don't want to dwell on the poems I didn't find rewarding, because really there's such a range of material here that practically any reader will come away instructed. Barron and Selinger admit that they could not be "inclusive of all the fine Jewish American poets currently writing," but they've done a fine job of getting in *something* from almost every shade of the spectrum. It's wholly appropriate that they've given the poets themselves a crack at theorizing Jewish American poetry; on the whole, they do a somewhat more lively job of it than the critics in the book's second section, "Reflections."

David Bleich's "Learning, Learning, Learning: Jewish Poetry in America" kicks off the "Reflections" section, and instead of starting this round with fancy footwork or a sharp left hook, Barron and Selinger have led with their editorial chins. Bleich is a genial enough voice, and pleasant to read, but let's face it—this essay doesn't contribute anything much to the discussion. Bleich rather disarmingly admits toward the end of his essay that he's "one of those who don't read much poetry." That comes as no surprise to anyone who's read thus far. His poetic examples seem to have been plucked randomly from anthologies, and his chief theoretical source (and source of his title) is Alan Dershowitz (!). How does one spend three pages on Kaddish-poems by American Jews with nary a mention of Allen Ginsberg's single greatest work? (My own preference, frankly, would have been to get something from a Language poet or critic of Language poetry to fill Bleich's space—but having edited a critical collection myself, and thereby knowing just how difficult it is to solicit work and ride herd on multiple contributors, I can only quote a pretty good non-Jewish poet: "You can't always get what you want.")

Things get better rapidly. Steven J. Rubin's "Poets of the Promised Land: 1800–1920" is a detailed history of the first century or so of Jewish American poetry, and provides a badly-needed fleshing out of the literary history provided in the editors' introduction. Michael Heller's "Diasporic Poetics" provides both a compact and sensitive history of the Objectivist movement—Louis Zukofsky, George Oppen, Carl Rakosi, Charles Reznikoff—and a thoughtful meditation of how those poets shaped Heller's own poetry and his attitude toward Jewishness. It's a nice piece, drawing on Heller's memoir *Living Root* and building on his volume of essays on the Objectivists, *Conviction's Net of Branches*.

The editors weigh in next, Selinger with a three-ring circus of an essay on the figure of the Shekhinah in some recent American poets, which he proffers as the "down payment" on "a rangy omnivorous book to be written on the strange career of Shekhinah in America." (He's got at least one reader hooked, I'll add.) Barron's essay on "Commentary in Contemporary Jewish American Poetry" advances a fascinating thesis, that American Jewish poets have responded to the fundamentally Christian theological tradition of the English lyric by producing against-the-grain, subversive commentaries on that tradition. Well and good, but no matter what marvels of midrash Barron applies to Maxine Kumin's "Living Alone with Jesus," he still can't convince me that this rather pallid little poem's language has managed simultaneously to subvert Deep Image, Confessional, and

Projectivist poetics. Maeera Shreiber's "A Flair for Deviation: The Troublesome Potential of Jewish Poetics" contains a whole against-the-grain history of Jewish poetry in kernel, and her sensitive reading of Jacqueline Osherow's "Moses in Paradise" ends up, like Selinger, thinking about the Shekhinah. One senses a critical groundswell of interest building in this ambiguous figure.

The next two essays, Janet Kaufman's on Jewish American women's poetry and Diane Matza's on Sephardic American poetry, seem, like the book's introduction, to be covering too much in too little space. I meet new poets in each of these essays, but come away with little sense of either field as a whole. Especially in the case of Kaufman's essay, which covers poets as diverse as Muriel Rukeyser and Jane Shore, I feel like I'm reading a compact travel guide to an entire continent. As traveller, I'd rather have the *Rough Guide* to Venice than *Let's Go Europe*.

The collection ends with two essays on language and Jewish poetry. John Felstiner's biography and translations of Paul Celan, already classics, have made that ill-starred master come to life to readers of English as no earlier versions could. His essay "Jews Translating Jews" is a wide-ranging, beautifully written (and all too short) meditation on translation and Jewish poetry, darting deftly between the historical and the mystical. "Translation," Felstiner quotes Walter Benjamin, "kindles from the endless renewal of languages as they grow to the messianic end of their history." In "*Di feder fun harts*/The Pen of the Heart: *Tsveyshprakhikayt*/Bilingualism and American Jewish Poetry" the poet Irena Klepfisz examines her own relationship to Yiddish, and recounts the various decisions that led her to write a bilingual Yiddish/English poetry. Where Felstiner writes in lofty, *ex cathedra* tones, Klepfisz is brisk and realistic, speaking hard truths about the contemporary status of Yiddish and the politics of Jewish American literature. "Communal Jewish prizes (and praise)," says Klepfisz, "support Jewish unity, survival, continuity. They would perhaps be self-destructive if they didn't. Nevertheless, such validation of a specific kind of Jewish literature inevitably censors or discourages another." Klepfisz writes as a lesbian and a supporter of the Intifada—and as someone who's never won a Jewish Book Award. But setting aside for the moment questions of *real* politics, one can rejoice that the last sentence of this quote, to the extent that it can be bent to apply to Jewish American *poetry* in general, is no longer true: the long critical eclipse of Jewish American poetry seems to be coming to an end, and Barron and Selinger's collection is one of the places from which new critics of that poetry will inevitably start.

Passionate, Eccentric Reading

Norman Finkelstein, *Not One of Them in Place: Modern Poetry and Jewish American Identity* (State University of New York Press, 2001)

The average reader-on-the-street, asked to name some prominent Jewish American writers, will probably still come up at least one of the Hart, Schaffner, and Marx of the Canon—Roth, Bellow, and Malamud. Yiddishists will invoke Isaac Bashevis Singer; critical theorists Harold Bloom, or perhaps Stanley Fish; and more adventurous readers will call up Cynthia Ozick. But where, among these masterful names, is a poet? Jewish American literature, until very recently, has constructed its canon not merely on the basis of ethnicity, but on the basis of genre as well, and prose fiction and commentary have reigned supreme. It seems that this is beginning to change. Following hard on the heels of Steven J. Rubin's anthology *Telling and Remembering: A Century of American Jewish Poetry* and Barron and Selinger's collection *Jewish American Poetry*, Norman Finkelstein's *Not One of Them in Place* is yet another sign that scholars of Jewish American literature are beginning to consider the work of American Jewish poets as specifically Jewish poetry.

American Jewish poetry is not quite coeval with American poetry as a whole—Emma Lazarus, the first notable poet in the tradition, is something of a latecomer relative to Emerson, Whitman, and the other poets of the "American Renaissance"—but over the course of the twentieth century Jewish poets have been prominent figures in the American poetic landscape: Gertrude Stein and Louis Zukofsky among the modernists; Muriel Rukeyser, Karl Shapiro, and Allen Ginsberg in midcentury; and, among a whole host of contemporaries, Albert Goldbarth, Marilyn Hacker, John Hollander, Jacqueline Osherow, Bob Perelman, and Marge Piercy. This spectacular flowering of talent—indeed, the absolutely central role of Jews in twentieth-century American poetry—makes all the more frustrating the almost exclusive attention critics have paid to Jewish American prose.

Finkelstein's study is of course in part an attempt to set the balance right, but it's as importantly an attempt—both explicit and implicit—to construct a working genealogy for contemporary American Jewish poetry. Finkelstein's genealogy, like all genealogies, is selective, and focuses on the Objectivist poets of the 1930s—Charles Reznikoff and Louis Zukofsky in particular—and a selection of poets active in the second half of the century whose work has clear continuities with the Objectivists: Finkelstein discusses Jerome Rothenberg and Armand Schwerner under Rothenberg's category of "ethnopoetics," while he talks about Harvey Shapiro, Michael Heller, and Hugh Seidman more explicitly as "a second generation of Jewish New Yorkers writing in the Objectivist mode." Needless to say, this isn't a family tree of Jewish American poetry that will please everyone. Finkelstein calls himself "a passionate, if rather eccentric reader," and it's worth noting that he is himself a poet of great gifts (and by no means to be confused with the much-reviled radical historian Norman G. Finkelstein, author of *The Holocaust Industry*). As he puts it in his preface, "I have never abandoned my faith in the category of the aesthetic," and it's clear throughout *Not One of Them in Place*, even as Finkelstein engages issues of sociology, literary history, and theology, that he is concerned as well with defining poetics that can prove viable for contemporary writers—that he seeks, in Wallace Stevens's words, "what will suffice" as a starting point for poetries of this new century.

The Objectivist tradition in which Finkelstein is so heavily invested is (by his account) a peculiarly Jewish development of the high modernist poetics of Eliot, Pound, and William Carlos Williams. The Objectivist poem, in the hands of its most notable makers—Zukofsky, Reznikoff, George Oppen—is a spare, taut, free-verse artifact, emphasizing image over rhetoric, observation over emotion, sharp juxtaposition over rhetorical continuity. It's the antithesis of the Romantic lyric. As one might expect, such a poetry has few attractions for such a self-styled Romantic as Harold Bloom, and Bloom is in part the dark angel of Finkelstein's study. In his 1972 essay, "The

Sorrows of American-Jewish Poetry," Bloom weighed the Objectivist mode in his critical balances and found it wanting, unable to carry the burden of the high poetic destiny to which American Jewish poets (like all good post-Romantics) ought to aspire. Finkelstein rightly rejects this prescriptive, totalizing view of modern poetry, enlisting as ally Marjorie Perloff, whose 1985 essay "Pound/Stevens: whose era?" divides twentieth-century American poetry into "constructivist" and Romanticist or Symbolist modes. Perloff demonstrates compellingly how fundamental presuppositions about the aims and nature of poetry make it literally impossible for Romanticist critics like Bloom, Hollander, and Helen Vendler to evaluate the works of the high modernists, the Objectivists, and their descendants.

Finkelstein is nothing if not a generous reader, however, and one of his most engaging chapters is devoted to Allen Grossman, a poet squarely within Bloom's tradition, and whose "theophoric" (god-bearing) poetics provide a model of Jewish American poetry much at odds with the other writers treated in *Not One of Them in Place*. All of the individual readings in this book, in fact, are generous, intelligent, and revealing. One might single out for particular praise the treatment of Louis Zukofsky, where Finkelstein reads Zukofsky, the Yiddish-speaking ghetto child who would go on to develop an almost uncanny mastery of the entire English-language literary tradition, in contrast to his contemporaries, the Yiddish-language poets of the Inzikhist (Introspectivist) movement (Jacob Glatshteyn, A. Leyeles, N. B. Minkov). Or Finkelstein's career overview of Zukofsky's former student Hugh Seidman, an astonishingly moving poet whose work has received almost no critical attention whatsoever.

All of the more recent poets Finkelstein discusses—Seidman, Heller, Shapiro, Schwerner, and Rothenberg—have been sorely underserved by the critical community, in fact. Finkelstein's study, concise, elegant, and lucidly written, ought to begin a more vigorous critical conversation about some of this past century's—and our new century's—most interesting poets. At the same time, it demonstrates that the discussion of Jewish American poetry, though still in its infancy, has attained an impressive intellectual maturity and depth.

BY THE RIVERS OF BABYLON

Maeera Y. Shreiber, *Singing in a Strange Land: A Jewish American Poetics* (Stanford University Press, 2007)

The opening of Psalm 137, a lament of the Children of Israel in Babylonian exile, is one of the most justly famous passages in the Hebrew Bible: "By the rivers of Babylon, there we sat down, yea, we wept, when we remembered Zion.... there they that carried us away captive required of us a song; and they that wasted us required of us mirth, saying, Sing us one of the songs of Zion. How shall we sing the LORD's song in a strange land?" Maeera Shreiber's study of Jewish American poetry takes its title from this passage, and its overall conceptual framework of Jewish poetry as a lyric discourse produced from within a condition of exile. "The notion of poetry (the act of singing in a strange land) as both a response to and a consequence of exile, a condition of radical displacement," Shreiber writes, "is particularly relevant to the condition of modern Jewish American verse." Indeed, she contends, "exile becomes the master narrative in which all Jewish poems begin"; and perhaps more cynically, "radical displacement," for the twentieth-century Jewish American poet, "turns out to be a real aesthetic boon."

The notion of Jewish writing as inherently exilic is by no means a new one, and Shreiber is acutely aware of earlier thinkers along these lines, from the melancholy dialectics of Theodor Adorno's Minima Moralia, written in exile in California, to George Steiner's essay "Our Homeland, the Text," as well as such further considerations on exile as the Palestinian Edward Said's essays. Indeed, the notion of poetry in general as based in displacement is a common trope: witness Polish poet Czeslaw Milosz's statement "Language is the only homeland," or the Luxembourg-born poet Pierre Joris's persistent meditations on the poet's transitional state. In some sense, however, the Jewish people's exile—first in Babylonian captivity, then in the Roman-enforced diaspora—is the archetypal exile, a displacement that has resonated throughout Western culture.

Jewish American writing has received a great deal of critical attention, and while historically much of that attention has been focused on the works of fiction writers and essayists, Jewish American poetry has more recently begun to be examined with the sort of specific care that has hitherto been reserved for Bellow, Ozick, and Roth. Shreiber's is perhaps one of the last books that needs even to nod toward the critical neglect the genre has suffered. What sets Shreiber's book apart from many contemporary studies of Jewish American writing is her refusal to regard Jewishness as a purely ethnic category (along the lines of "Asian American" or "African American"). Instead, she insists that Judaism as *religion*, as faith-system, must be considered an integral part of any definition of what "Jewish American poetry" might mean. Shreiber is well equipped to examine the religious traditions behind the poetries she examines; her book shows evidence of an encyclopedic knowledge of the Hebrew Bible, the various Jewish liturgical traditions, and the Midrashic commentaries, and she brings this knowledge to bear in telling and sometimes surprising ways.

Poetry, according to Shreiber, is "a dramatic site in which the intersections of culture, history, and theology come into striking relief," and her readings of the historical backgrounds of the poets and poetries she discusses are invariably illuminating. Even more so is her reading of culture, in particular the gendering of the Jewish tradition, and how that tradition has in turn gendered the poetic voice. This is particularly highlighted in Chapter Four, which examines how Adrienne Rich attempts to refigure the "lament," an ancient rhetorical form traditionally assigned to the feminine voice, and thereby traditionally devalued. Throughout, Shreiber reminds us of the figure of "the Shekinah, the kabbalistic term for the feminine figuration of the Godhead," and specifically the aspect of the deity which accompanies the Jewish people in their exile.

The poets treated in *Singing in a Strange Land* range across the twentieth century and into the twenty-first. In her first chapter, Shreiber sets the terms for the discussion of Jewish American poetry in general, and examines how Emma Lazarus, in the anthology piece "The New Colossus," attempts to refigure the site of Jewish homecoming in the American New World. In the second chapter, she examines the perennial figure of the "Jewish mother" in Charles Reznikoff and Allen Ginsberg, showing how each of those poets refuses the stereotypical denigration of that figure in the process of negotiating the persistent social gendering of his own art as feminine. Chapter Three, "'Speaking About Epics,'" reads the Objectivist poets Louis Zukofsky and George Oppen in terms of their relationship with history, and with the "epic" tradition that they inherited most proximately from such high modernists as Ezra Pound; Zukofsky and Oppen, in Shreiber's nuanced reading, refuse the ethnic "collective" upon which epic history is traditionally built: they find that the narrative of exile "proves to be the cornerstone of a coercive model of belonging, and thus at odds with less prescriptive, more open structures of community."

The real heart of the book lies in its last two chapters, which explore the relationship between (secular) poetry and prayer. In "'Unreachable Father': Exploring the Boundary Between Poetry and Prayer," Shreiber pauses briefly on Marcia Falk's rather wan attempts at updating the *Siddur* (prayer-book), then lingers on Oppen's "Psalm," a poem which asserts "faith" in the connection between language and the natural world, before conducting a full-scale reading of Louise Glück's *The Wild Iris* as a re-visioning both of prayer and of the Edenic narrative. For Shreiber, what is crucial about prayer in the Jewish tradition is that it is an address not to a commensurate subjectivity, but to a wholly other (she invokes Levinas at a couple of points), and any conception of poetry as prayer that falls short of this falls back into the traditional model of self-centered Romantic subjectivity.

Indeed, the poet upon whom *Singing in a Strange Land* settles as the strongest and strangest model of a poetry not as prayer, but as preamble to prayer, is Allen Grossman, whose book *How to Do*

Things with Tears receives a pointed reading in the final chapter, "'Do Not Be Content with an Imaginary God.'" Grossman's model of a "theophoric" (god-bearing) poetics, a poetry in which the poet renounces all aspirations toward self-expression and originality in order to carry *truth* itself, emerges as the most essentially *Jewish* of the various poetics treated in the book as a whole.

Shreiber is a strong and sensitive reader of poetry, and shows a refreshing eclecticism of taste in the poets she chooses to discuss (who would have imagined both Louis Zukofsky and Louise Glück receiving such intelligent readings between the same covers?). Her intimate knowledge of Jewish religious texts and cultural traditions, however, makes *Singing in a Strange Land* more than just another volume of literary criticism: it is itself a cultural intervention of rare strength and insight, and will advance the reading of Jewish American poetry, and Jewish American writing in general, to a new level of theological and cultural sophistication.

ZUK AND OLE BILL

The Correspondence of William Carlos Williams and Louis Zukofsky, edited by Barry Ahearn (Wesleyan University Press, 2003)

William Carlos Williams's reputation among twentieth-century American writing, it would seem, is assured; that of his younger friend Louis Zukofsky, while apparently on the rise, is less well-established. Williams's work—loving in its sympathy for the quotidien, impatient of formal constraints, sexually profluent, vividly *alive*—is, like the poet himself, immediately likeable. In contrast to the physician-poet whose works appear in high school classrooms and graduate syllabi alike, Zukofsky comes across as a torture-master of syntax; a weaver of Gordian Knots of arcane personal and literary reference; an emotionally arid technician of line and sound. That impression, I would argue, doesn't do justice to the body of Zukofsky's work; equally unfair is the notion that he is to be read merely as an epigone of Ezra Pound's, extending, complicating, and playing variations upon Pound's techniques. That the only extended selection of Zukofsky's correspondence previously available has been Barry Ahearn's *Pound/Zukofsky: Selected Letters of Ezra Pound and Louis Zukofsky* has no doubt served to perpetuate the latter misreading of Zukofsky. One of the great values of Ahearn's edition of the Williams/Zukofsky correspondence is that it shows Zukofsky in a new light, that of his thirty-five year relationship with Williams. But the light these letters cast upon Zukofsky's career is complemented and even outshone by the illumination in which they place Williams's.

In short, it is good a very good thing to have the correspondence between Williams and Zukofsky in print, especially in such a conscientiously, even loving prepared edition. Ahearn has approached his task with an unparalleled knowledge of both poets' lives and careers, and his annotations to the letters are bibliographically precise and scrupulously informative. This volume prints all of the surviving correspondence: 565 cards and letters from Williams to Zukofsky,

161 from Zukofsky to Williams. Zukofsky, it is clear, was far more careful to preserve his letters received—one index of how important the correspondence with Williams was to him. But while Williams may not have saved all of Zukofsky's letters, his letters to the younger poet underline how crucial Zukofsky's friendship became over the last thirty-five years of Williams's life.

Twenty years younger than Williams, Zukofsky got in touch with the older poet in 1928 at Ezra Pound's instigation: "go down an' stir up ole Bill Willyums.... He is still the best human value on my murkn. visiting list." The two poets—one in Rutherford, the other in New York City—would become fast friends and close literary collaborators. Zukofsky constantly showed his work to Williams, and Williams came to prize Zukofsky as an invaluable sounding board and editor, from *The Descent of Winter* (1928)—which is Zukofsky's selection from a mass of Williams's manuscripts—to *The Wedge* (1944), which reflects Zukofsky's blue-pencilling as much as *The Waste Land* did Ezra Pound's. Though their friendship suffered a temporary lapse in the mid-Thirties in connection with Zukofsky and his friend Tibor Serly's work on Williams's opera *The First President*, the two poets remained on close and warm terms to the end of Williams's life.

Poets' letters at their best teach us something about poetry itself, about the creative processes that result in the finished texts that we ponder, study, and sometimes love. But even when the writing of poems is near the center of a human being's life, the bulk of that life is apt to be occupied with more mundane matters: love, marriage, and domesticity, making a living, suffering inclement weather, negotiating a mortgage. Of Keats's letters, so widely held up as central documents in English poetics, probably no more than a dozen pages all told cast real light on Keats's poetry. It is refreshing, then, to find how much of the Williams/Zukofsky correspondence has an actual bearing on the two men's writings.

True, a dauntingly large proportion of the items—by number, not by length—consists of the communications of two men separated by some miles and without a steady telephone line: invitations to dinner in Rutherford or proposed meetings in the city, repeatedly cancelled and rescheduled. There is much talk, not of poetry, but of the *business* of poetry. The young Zukofsky would spend some fifteen years trying to find a publisher for a book of his poems, while early in their correspondence Williams was more than happy to let Zukofsky try to find magazine homes for Williams's own scripts. The two men argued over and plotted possible magazine projects and putative "movements" (one of this collection's minor revelations is how much the rhetoric of Zukofsky's early "Objectivist" manifestos owes to passing statements in Williams's letters). They wrote commentaries on each others' work, and then brainstormed as to which magazines might print them.

And there are the events of everyday life, of the mature poet observing his sons growing up, marrying, going to war, and having children of their own, his medical practice fluctuating, his reputation gradually growing; of the younger poet scrabbling through the 1930s to find steady work, marrying and settling down in Brooklyn Heights, nurturing the early career of his violin-virtuoso son Paul, and fulminating—not constantly, but with quiet passive-aggressive persistence—about his own lack of public recognition. These letters are obviously a rich source of biographical information about the two poets: there is scarcely a page of Paul Mariani's overlong biography *William Carlos Williams: A New World Naked* that is not marked by his consultation of the Williams-Zukofsky correspondence.

But whatever directions the two men's lives took, poetry remained their central bond, and a gratifyingly significant proportion of their letters consists of discussion of particular poems—usually each others'—rather than the mechanics of the poetry industry. Much of this discussion is of a "workshop" nature: suggestions of possible revisions, queries about the meaning of a particular phrase or the "rightness" of a particular line—precisely the sort of minute interventions into another's work that best shows a poet's critical intelligence at work.

Zukofsky tended to mark up and return the scripts Williams sent him, so there are comparatively few comments by Zukofsky on specific poems (though Zukofsky does write at some length about his general impressions of Williams's work and its direction). Williams, in contrast, would return Zukofsky's poems and comment upon them in the covering letters, so that we have a rather full record of his reaction to his friend's work. Notable, for instance, are Williams's comments on the first (later heavily revised) movement of the long poem *"A"* (20 December 1928), and his reaction to Zukofsky's sestina "'Mantis'" (20 October 1934), portions of which Zukofsky incorporated into that poem's sequel, "'Mantis,' An Interpretation."

From the beginning, Williams found Zukofsky's poetry tough going—in his first comment on Zukofsky's work, he described it as "thoughtful poetry, but actual word stuff, not thoughts for thoughts," and noted that "It escapes me in the analysis"—but he remained convinced of his friend's intelligence and poetic potential, even if the latter often seemed overwhelmed by the former in the actual poems. Zukofsky was something of an enigma to Williams: a younger colleague who shared his passionate commitment to revitalizing American poetry, a fellow-laborer in the hard and unrewarding enterprise of the new; the possessor of an immensely useful critical eye, who often seemed to understand what Williams was up to better than Williams himself; but a poet whose actual writings all too often seemed tangled up in conceptualities. "[W]hat disturbs me most," Williams wrote to Zukofsky about the poems of *Anew* (1946), "is the lack of emotional impact. I am repelled by the impenetrability of the words—or the words that just ain't there, to my ears. I don't know what the hell to say. Your poems make my own work <seem> juvenile, considered as constructions. I nevertheless come away baffled."

Williams's mixed feelings about Zukofsky's poetry persist as an undercurrent through much of their correspondence, but fall away for one incandescent moment in 1958, when Williams—ill from another stroke—finally got around to reading Zukofsky's mid-length poem

"4 Other Countries": "I don't care if I never write another line and hope not to do it after Floss has just read me the 4 Other Countries which she has just finished reading me and at her own request reading it over again.... You have come through this once. I will hold you to this for the rest of my life. And as I say I hope never to write a word gain, a word of poetry, as long as I shall live. There is enough in this poem to occupy me for years or according to my determination forever." Zukofsky's faith in Williams's work had never wavered, and this late recognition on Williams's part could only have heartened him, though bittersweetly. These letters chart the history of American poetry in the twentieth century as embodied in the careers of two major poets, but they speak to us more immediately as they chart the course of a fraught but intense friendship between two men of great talents but disparate sensibilities.

A Poetics of Being

Peter Nicholls, *George Oppen and the Fate of Modernism* (Oxford University Press, 2007)

It is a banner moment for George Oppen scholarship. On the heels of Michael Davidson's beautifully edited and revelatory edition of Oppen's *New Collected Poems* (New Directions, 2002), the past two years have seen the publication of Lyn Graham Barzilai's *George Oppen: A Critical Study* (McFarland, 2006), Michael Heller's *Speaking the Estranged: Essays on the Work of George Oppen* (Salt, 2008), and Stephen Cope's edition of Oppen's *Selected Prose, Daybooks, and Papers* (University of California Press, 2007). Peter Nicholls's *George Oppen and the Fate of Modernism* is perhaps the most significant of these publications, at least in terms of Oppen's standing within the American and British academies: it is the first full-length, single-author study devoted entirely to Oppen to be published by a major academic press, and in this it is comparable to such landmark works as Stephen Fredman's Reznikoff study, *A Menorah for Athena*, Peter Makin's *Bunting: The Shaping of His Verse*, or even Hugh Kenner's *The Poetry of Ezra Pound*. Oppen's standing within the community of poets and of poetry readers, one hastens to add, has never been in doubt: among his Objectivist contemporaries, Oppen seems to have been the most successful in attracting devoted readers from all quarters of the severely balkanized poetic community.

I had heard rumors for a couple of years that Nicholls—whose *Ezra Pound: Economics and Writing* (1984) and *Modernisms: A Literary Guide* (1995) are eminently useful, sometimes ground-breaking works—was writing a biography of Oppen, and I was enthusiastically awaiting the book for reasons both personal and professional. It turns out that *George Oppen and the Fate of Modernism*, though it includes much newly revealed biographical information and is organized along chronological lines, is not a biography, but a career-wide study of Oppen's poetry and poetics. It is also a thesis-driven work: Nicholls's thesis is that Oppen's own brand of Objectivist poetics, while it may early on bear some superficial resemblance to Pound's modernism, reveals itself as a highly personal poethics (Joan Retallack's term) that rejects both the traditionalism of a Poundian/Eliotian "high" modernism and the ultimately apolitical (in Nicholls's account) avant-gardism of such groups as the Language Poets: "Somewhere between these" alternatives, Nicholls writes, Oppen believed that "the poet might discover something truly original—a poetics of being, I have called it—that was not reducible to either a myth of the past or to stylistic experimentation masquerading as politics."

As Eliot Weinberger remarks in the Preface to the *New Collected Poems*, Oppen "may never be the subject of a biography, for his life beyond its outline remains a mystery, and for decades left no paper trail." This may turn out true (though writers with lives far more scantily documented than Oppen's have proved the subject of triumphant biographies), but Nicholls, as he traces Oppen's poetic career, goes some way toward dispelling the notion that Oppen is a man without a record. His pages on the Oppens' years of exile in Mexico cast new light on the stretch of Oppen's adulthood between his active years of Leftist organizing and his return to poetry; the community of American political exiles in Mexico City, it turns out, was substantial and rather illustrious, including Dalton Trumbo, Ring Lardner Jr., the composer Conlon Nancarrow, and even a cousin of Louis Zukofsky's.

Though he provides a thumbnail running commentary on Oppen's life and career, the years in Mexico and the Oppens' 1975 trip to Israel are the only biographical moments upon which Nicholls lingers. Significantly, these are the moments in Oppen's life that have perhaps attracted the most speculation, and Nicholls sheds grateful light upon them. But the biography Nicholls is most interested in is not the record of the external events of Oppen's life, but the narrative of his intellectual and poetic development, and it's here that *George Oppen and the Fate of Modernism* proves itself most valuable. Simply put, as an account of the development of Oppen's poetics and of the influences on his thought, and as a series of illustrative readings of some of his most important poems, Nicholls's book is an exemplary piece of scholarship.

One always has cavils. I can't help feeling that Nicholls tends to oversimplify the difficulties of Oppen's poetry, to minimize the ambiguities of syntax and reference that puzzle the ordinary reader. He's liable to haul in extratextual evidence—the Daybooks, letters, interviews—to gloss knotty passages in the poetry, without reflecting on how the verse might be construed without such aids. He pays rather too little attention to the formal aspects of the poetry: the lineation and spacing, the attenuated syntax, the expressive linebreaks. At the one point where Nicholls engages in a full-dress formal argument regarding the function of caesurae in Oppen's late poetry, I find myself quite unconvinced: scansion is no doubt an art rather than a science, but I can't find the systematic use of caesura that Nicholls brings Maurice Blanchot in to illuminate.

And while he makes deft use of Oppen's correspondence, both published and unpublished, Nicholls perhaps pays too little attention to Oppen's interactions with his correspondents and his contemporaries, instead tracing his poetic and intellectual development largely through his reading. It gives us—perhaps inadvertently—an image of Oppen as an overwhelmingly *bookish* poet, more immersed in Hegel and Heidegger than in his conversations with Robert Duncan and the young Rachel Blau.

But it's Nicholls's scrupulous tracing of Oppen's reading that really makes *George Oppen and the Fate of Modernism* a scholarly triumph (and, one might add, a rather obsessively readable book, at least for a library-cormorant like myself). Nicholls it seems has read every book that Oppen ever mentioned; he's been through Oppen's own library, searching for markings and annotations; and—perhaps most importantly—he's examined Oppen's reading on the basis of the volumes and editions Oppen himself used, which tend to be a scrappy and unscholarly lot. Nicholls is able to show, for instance, that

Oppen's mature fascination with Hegel can be narrowed down to a single sentence from the Preface to *The Phenomenology of Spirit*, found not in the "standard" Baillie translation but in Walter Kaufmann's *Hegel: Reinterpretation, Texts, and Commentary* (1965), which includes a translation of the Preface: Oppen probably never read any further into the *Phenomenology*. For his purposes as poet, that single sentence was enough.

Nor, for all of Oppen's investment in Heidegger, does Nicholls find any evidence that Oppen read *Being and Time* with any sustained attention. But the poet did read many of Heidegger's essays and shorter works, and Nicholls provides a dazzlingly specific account of precisely which Heidegger books Oppen owned, read, and referred to, and they made their way into his poems. Indeed, *George Oppen and the Fate of Modernism* is sprinkled with sharp aperçus regarding the relationship of Oppen's reading to his writings, the sorts of illuminations that bespeak long, shortcut-free hours in the archives.

Poets have taken Oppen's work very seriously indeed for some four decades now. In its combination of verbal precision, moral rigor, social commitment, and philosophical density, it has few rivals in twentieth-century American poetry. Peter Nicholls's *George Oppen and the Fate of Modernism*, one hopes, is a sign that the American and British academies have begun to take Oppen seriously as well.

SCARS AND FASCINATION

John Wilkinson, *Proud Flesh* (1986; Salt Publishing, 2005) and *Lake Shore Drive* (Salt Publishing, 2006)

Over the past three decades John Wilkinson has quietly established himself as one of England's most compelling poets. These two collections, bookending twenty years of Wilkinson's work, exemplify what makes his work—obdurate, knotty, at time repellant—so simultaneously fascinating and appalling.

"Proud flesh," the shorter OED tells us, is "Overgrown flesh arising from excessive granulation upon, or around the edge of, a healing wound." The poems of *Proud Flesh* are, appropriately, organic excrescences, verbal structures in response to physical trauma. The trauma, for the most part, involves one of the oldest lyric topoi: love. These are love poems, a strenuous, challenging, and often fruitfully disgusting reimagining of the lyric tradition of spiritual and erotic affection.

Wilkinson takes as axiomatic that the tradition of the love lyric has reached a point of exhaustion or impasse. He does not hesitate to graphically demonstrate how the tropes of love poetry reduce to metaphors, not of the poet's spirit, but of his body:

> Each metaphor sounds the same
> in its sepia, dry blood melancholy
>
> but if you cry, it drips blood
> onto the quarry tiles
>
> so you hasten for the authentic
> rasp of the next and the next
>
> leaving behind you dying homunculae

That blood-dripping cry evokes Blake's "hapless soldier's sight," which "runs in blood down palace walls," but here each new attempt at metaphor leaves behind it no more or less than a clot of abandoned sperm, "dying homunculae."

Like no other poetic text I know, *Proud Flesh* captures the extent to which romantic love plays itself out in a creaking and leaky labyrinth of plumbing through which pulse blood, mucus, sperm, and the more evanescent chemicals that lubricate the brain's CPU and its various nervous peripherals: "Under a mantelpiece my heart / horns pinch: and still born I drown in amniotic fluid."

Proud Flesh is at once a series of love poems and a clinical examination: Wilkinson does not hesitate to deploy the jawbreaking vocabulary of medical diagnosis, and at points his exploration of love's body becomes as savagely indignant as Swift's or Rochester's. Drawing on his experience as psychiatric nurse, Wilkinson is fascinated with the growth and structuring of the psyche itself, both in classic psychoanalytic terms and within the larger context of the subject's society:

> Slender pickings fall to the lap of the foster-child
> who chides them into their own spheres, the nuclei
> of unshockable plasm, home like everything he touches
> will be compèred by the memories they create before
>
> dust settles, spawn begins to heave. Is he socially
> acceptable? Does he use a knife and fork with facility?
> Will he boil his underwear, when living in the world
> where prompts are few? Do you rate his speech lucid?
>
> does he spill his life-blood over a phrase, and refuse
> to clear up? the quills he flurries from his spine
> thread these poor facts of life, draw them out and turn
> the loops separately to tap his fluid. Any capsule

of love, any midnight pearl, has had him for a unique
sponsor to its quality, concocting in his parietal
lobe a cool romance. There, for this gaunt clarity
its positive was pressed to a dilapidated back-yard.

The poem invites us to read the entire collection as a history of the subject's simultaneous initiation into society, into affective relationships and sexual desire, and into an almost Yeatsian longing for a state of sensual and aesthetic stasis, figured here as a "pearl"—the beautiful translucent object the oyster creates in response to physical discomfort—and figured through the rest of the collection as the frozen physical gesture of statuary: "Marble stains with the tears shed for it / Sperm shatters on its thighs."

Written twenty years after *Proud Flesh*, the poems of Wilkinson's latest collection *Lake Shore Drive* are more accessible, while remaining compacted, challenging, and deeply energetic. Where *Proud Flesh* focused upon the damage inflicted upon the subject by love, desire, and the cultural regimes of human coupling, *Lake Shore Drive* is obsessed with the whole bloody mess of contemporary culture, from the intractible, agonizing violence of the Palestinian/Israeli conflict—

> bonds mature
> between emplacements
> and holy writ,
> between the settlers and
> inflated psalms
> ****
> to the burnt offerings of capitalist consumerism:
> I like it sweet, I like it whipped, I like it salted,
>   I like it fresh-churned.
> Does the rose bush burnt from pure longing
>   visited with fire rust,
> transfigure in the blaze to the same figure?

> The same shall furl and pack fire
> into its prolific heads,
> and does the blood-red garland
>   decked in thorns like spurs,
>
> manifest the crowning dream of a virgin
> wading through blood—Don't fuck with me:
> I want the thick cultivar.
> The sentence is delayed hunger.

Lake Shore Drive is built around four sequences, "Cité Sportif," "Multistorey," "Iphigenia," and "Marram..." ("Marram Riff," "Marram Grass," etc.), each of which plays intense variations on a theme of human damage, whether physical, psychic, or cultural. They are at times almost unbearable, but I keep returning to them, marvelling at the strenuous energy of Wilkinson's syntax, the lyrical music of his lines, the impacted density of his images, and the constantly renewed surprise of his vocabulary. A bleak repugnancy and fascination, drawing me to a poetry that presents itself as some contemporary harpies' banquet—lush and abundant, continually befouled and snatched away:

> gull-shrieks of fury, custom-
>   crammed between
> rubbled minarets and domes,
> attend the Eucharistic table shit-spattered.

Resignation and Independence

Robert Archambeau, *The Poet Resigns: Poetry in a Difficult World* (University of Akron Press, 2013)

Poet who are also critics have been around for a long time: think Jonson, Dryden, Samuel Johnson. But if you don't mind my slipping into Robert Archambeau's preferred historico-sociological mode for a moment, it's evident that the poet-critic in the contemporary sense—the faculty poet, writing prose essays and criticism so that (or with the effect that) less poetical tenure and promotion committees have something to discuss—is largely a twentieth-century phenomenon, to be correlated with the professionalization of English studies in the middle third of the century and the rise of the Creative Writing Industry in the second half.

Archambeau himself, as he details in the "Letter of Resignation" that introduces *The Poet Resigns*, is a poet-critic in recovery, a poet who's found his energies shifting over the years from writing poetry to writing about poetry. And of course he's not entirely comfortable with that shift, so in a wholly characteristic manner he sets out to analyze it, most notably in "Oppen/Rimbaud: The Poet as Quitter," a meditation on two poets who also gave up poetry (Oppen for a quarter-century, Rimbaud permanently). His conclusions, that Rimbaud's abandonment of poetry was a logical next step in his poetic career as "escape artist," while Oppen elected to make the relationship of poetry to the world of power—precisely what had originally put him off poetry—the thematic center of his later work, seem to me spot-on.

The shades of Oppen and Rimbaud stalk through much of *The Poet Resigns*: Rimbaud, the intransigently avant-garde Communard sympathizer who abandoned poetry for gun-running; Oppen, who bailed out of the Objectivist "movement" (and poetry itself) in order to organize strikes for the American Communist Party. The two men are as it were limit-texts for the collision of poetry and active politics. But in their wake there have been whole generations of poets, in both Rimbaudian and Oppenian genealogies of influence, who have argued that making poems can be in itself a way of doing political labor. Archambeau's subtitle, "Poetry in a Difficult World," evokes Adrienne Rich (*An Atlas of the Difficult World*): where Rich's poems aim to examine and perhaps even to intervene in a world of disquiet, cruelty, and injustice, Archambeau is interested in the place poets stake out for their art, the claims they make about the relationship of poetry and power—and the motivations for such claims.

The primary tools Archambeau uses to prise open the stories poets tell about their work's place in the world are good old-fashioned historical perspective, combined with a heady dose of sociological analysis. (Archambeau's sociology is inflected by that of Pierre Bourdieu, but it's often a quite common-sense questioning of the social roots of intellectual stances.) For instance, in "The Discursive Situation of Poetry," he examines the familiar genre of the "Lament over the Irrelevance of Poetry Today." We've all been through several rounds of this, from Dana Gioia's 1992 *Can Poetry Matter?* to whatever the latest screed is, and the general theme is familiar: once upon a time people read poetry, poetry mattered to a "general public," poetry was *important*. Who to blame for this state of affairs depends on your inclination: the rise of popular culture and the dumbing-down of America, those dratted modernists who made poetry a pedant's game, the MFA industry, and so forth.

It's all based, Archambeau convincingly argues, on the false premise that poets' possessing a kind of social importance is something other than a transient historical phenomenon. When Dana Gioia or Joseph Epstein or Mark Edmundson (most recently) evokes a golden age in which poetry mattered, what they're really thinking of is a very specific historical moment: the mid-nineteenth century, the age of Tennyson, of the Victorian Sage. A great time to be a poet or a Sage—but not so great to be an illiterate factory operative, who outnumbered the Sages by a rather large factor. If we want poets to matter the way Tennyson mattered, Archambeau points out, we need to return to the social conditions of 1850.

Wanting the poet to have the cultural stature of a Victorian Sage is an aspiration closely related to various poets' assertions of the political status of their work. Archambeau spends some serious time analyzing some of these assertions, teasing out the complex weave of Krishnamurti-like cultism and political self-aggrandizement among the poets associated with J. H. Prynne ("Public Faces in Private Places: Notes on Cambridge Poetry"), totting up some of the political claims made on behalf of Language Poetry ("The Aesthetic Anxiety: Avant-Garde Poetics and the Idea of Politics"), and presenting a pretty damning indictment of Charles Bernstein's insider-outsider claims about the poet in the academy ("The Poet in the University: Charles Bernstein's Academic Anxiety"). These essays (and several others on related topics) are smart, thoughtful, and written in a gratifyingly lucid prose. More importantly, they pose questions of context and motivation that very much need to be confronted. But as convinced as I am by Archambeau's analysis of the social roots of poets' desire to *matter* politically, I can't help feeling that he's given short shrift to the actual *content* of their political claims. Too often one gets the sense that for Archambeau, unless poetry literally "makes something happen" (to misquote Auden)—sends young people off to the barricades or packing to join the Abraham Lincoln Brigade, makes the Minister of the Interior resign in shame—then any political claims one makes for it are simply self-delusive. Archambeau does indeed take into account alternative propositions as to how poems might make a political or social difference, but he tends to dismiss them a trifle too hastily for my taste.

Sometimes, alas, the (recovering) poet-critic's socio-theoretical apparatus becomes unwieldy. When he trots out (with a drumroll) the still-resonant chestnut from Marx's *Critique of Political Economy* that "it is not the consciousness of men that determines their being, but, on the contrary, their social being that determines their consciousness," only to tell us that poets, having less investment than stockbrokers in immediate economic events, are inclined to take longer (more liberal) cultural views, I get the feeling that a rather large and complex theoretical machine has been deployed to crush a rather small butterfly. And too often Archambeau tends to erect an over-elaborate conceptual scaffolding over a puny excavation. It's true enough that we can call the Irish poet Gabriel Fitzgerald, who seems still to be working his way through the Easter Rebellion and the Celtic Twilight, something of a "decadent"—but wouldn't it be briefer, and even more fun, to simply point out how mawkish and incompetent his verses are?

Archambeau has written a study of the poets who studied with Yvor Winters at Stanford (Robert Pinsky, Robert Hass, James McMichael, John Matthias, and John Peck), *Laureates and Heretics*, and is at work on a large historical study of the notion of poetic autonomy from the eighteenth century to the present. In contrast, the pieces in *The Poet Resigns* are largely occasional—book reviews, responses to immediate controversies, expanded versions of Archambeau's thoughtful blog posts. And they have the advantage of the best occasional writing: immediacy, a sense of responsiveness, conversationality. But Archambeau is a "big ideas" critic: he invariably wants to spin his momentary interpretations of texts into larger insights about the place of poetry in the world. Sometimes, as in the more general essays in the first half of the book, this results in excellent and provocative meditations; sometimes individual poets, poems, and passages from poems become no more than grist for a relentless point-making mill.

There is enough to think about in *The Poet Resigns* to fill a shelf of books, and if Archambeau has the tendency sometimes to answer the big questions of our poetic moment rather more rapidly than I'm comfortable with, he's to be given abundant kudos for raising them in such a clear and thoughtful manner, and for tackling them in such lively and intelligent prose. There are many moments in *The Poet Resigns* when Archambeau's affection for poetry (in all of its forms) and his sensitive critical intelligence align perfectly with his structure-making impulses. And the more personal moments of this collection, such as the delightful "My Laureates," show that the poet-critic, whether his resignation be temporary or permanent, is by no means afraid to subject his own socio-politico-theoretical position to the same examination he has brought to bear on others.

Twilight Gardening

Ronald Johnson, *The Shrubberies*, edited by Peter O'Leary. Flood Editions, 2001.

> And the LORD God planted a garden eastward in Eden; and there he put the man whom he had formed.(Genesis 2.8)

> And Jacob went out from Beer-sheba, and went toward Haran. And he lighted upon a certain place, and tarried there all night, because the sun was set; and he took of the stones of that place, and put *them for* his pillows, and lay down in that place to sleep. And he dreamed, and behold a ladder set up on the earth, and the top of it reached to heaven: and behold the angels of God ascending and descending on it. (Genesis 28.10–12)

The Hebrew Bible begins with the Lord speaking into existence the world and all its creatures—the whole labyrinthine system of plant and animal life dependent, as the scientists tell us, on that first-created element, light—and placing the crown of his creation, the human being, into a garden containing the Tree of Life. At the end of the Christian Bible, St. John the Divine stands in awe at the vision of the New Jerusalem, where the Tree of Life—once again available to mankind—spreads its branches over the crystal purity of the river of the water of life.

In between these two astonishing moments, of course, a great deal of bad stuff takes place. Humanity is wiped out in a flood; cities are destroyed by fire and brimstone; kingdoms and empires are overthrown; good kings and bad kings alike come to untimely ends; martyrs are beaten and stoned. But there are also moments (too few, too far between) of transcendent vision, flashback to Eden or flashforward to the New Jerusalem.

The American poet Ronald Johnson, who died of a brain tumor in 1998, was one of the rare contemporaries who sought to preserve this visionary impulse in his poetry, to remain continually on one rung or another of Jacob's ladder. Johnson's early work, collected in *A Line of Poetry, A Row of Trees* (1964) and *Valley of the Many-Colored Grasses* (1969), used his midwestern background as a launching pad for energetic, Olsonian speculations on cultural origins, nature, and sexuality. *The Book of the Green Man* (1967), based on a walking tour of England and Wales, wove a Zukofskyan variety of source texts into a dazzling, brooding meditation on the interpenetration of natural processes and human culture.

All this, however—as well as the various little volumes of "concrete" poetry Johnson published through the Sixties and Seventies—was merely the wind-up for Johnson's big project, a epic-length cosmological poem that would occupy him for two decades. *ARK*, which Johnson began in 1970 and completed in 1990, is a 99-section poem in the tradition of Pound's *Cantos* and Zukofsky's *"A"*. Its notable difference from these modernist doorstops, however—in spite of all the similarities, from its mosaic, collagistic texture to its very ambition—is that *ARK* is, in Johnson's words, a poem (contra Pound) "*without* history." *ARK* is many things: a hymn to process, a paean to light, a series of interconnected visionary exfoliations of the "*fiat lux*." Above all else, it is an extended, high-spirited, ludic exploration of human language-making.

ARK is a beautiful book, and a grand achievement—for unlike Pound, Charles Olson, and William Carlos Williams, Johnson actually managed to bring his big project to completion. But where to go then? "Blocks to Be Arranged in a Pyramid," a poem of sixty-six dark, dense, but still visionary quatrains, was Johnson's memorial to the victims of AIDS, the plague that ravaged San Francisco through the Eighties. Johnson had lived most of his adult life in the Bay area. For a young gay man brought up in flat, repressive Kansas, San Francisco was indeed Oz, the Emerald City—a place of limitless beauty and color, of utter freedom both sexual and intellectual. (Imagery from Baum's *The Wizard of Oz* is woven throughout *ARK*, and constitutes, along with Noah's Ark and Orpheus and Eurydice, one of the poem's central myths.) But for the last few years of his life, the period during which Johnson wrote the poems of *The Shrubberies*, he was back in Kansas: grey, monochrome Kansas, with the eye-popping technicolor of Oz left far behind.

In increasingly ill health, Johnson lived with his father in Topeka and worked (in the words of Peter O'Leary, Johnson's literary executor and editor of *The Shrubberies*) "as a handyman, gardener, and occasional cook at Ward-Meade, an historic park in town." Cooking, of course, was Johnson's *métier*; he had managed and cooked for restaurants in the Bay area, and had written cookbooks among the very best in the genre. (*The American Table*, his masterpiece, has recently been reprinted by the Silver Spring Press.)

And gardening was one of the central metaphors of his poetry. BEAM 30 of *ARK*, subtitled "The Garden," begins with the line "'To do as Adam did,'" and this epitomizes much of Johnson's project in *ARK*: both to tend the garden and to give names to the creatures therein—in the context of the poem, to uncover the maze-like homologies of life, light, and physics, and to celebrate the human gift of word-making and word-play. Throughout *ARK*, Johnson sounds and re-sounds the theme of the poet as gardener, and the related theme of the garden—the *hortus inclusus*—as analogue to the human body, and microcosmic reflection of the whole interlinked system of the universe.

Where *ARK* is a massive, if home-made, monument, *The Shrubberies* are gardening on a far smaller scale. In these 120 short poems—none longer than a page and half, one a single line—Johnson's powers of verbal euphony, precise lineation, wistful wordplay, and visionary semantic leaping are brought to bear on isolated moments of thought and perception, isolated instances of perception. The chiming of words, for instance, evokes the shimmer of a dawn:

> sunrise like a radish
> pulled up beneath us

> this is the god Ra
> the orisons of Osiris
>
> lustrations of iris
> living white samite
>
> –shine upon shine
> sheen through sheen

Johnson's poems again and again plant miniature gardens, miniature labyrinths, in which the echoes of words evoke moments of visionary intensity such as T. S. Eliot experienced in the garden of Burnt Norton. "always my core dream," Johnson writes, "winding a garden / secret in every sense." Every *sense*, as in every meaning, but also all of the five human senses, and in addition the senses of myth, of history, tradition, and memory. *ARK* began quite explicitly as a long poem "without history," but the AIDS epidemic left its black fingerprints all over the second half of that poem, infusing the buildup to the visionary takeoff of "ARK 99, Arches XXXIII" with an unmistakeable residuum of loss.

That same loss is everywhere evident in *The Shrubberies*. While the garden may be a microcosm cultivated by the poet—in one poem, Johnson's desk is "cleared for planting"—it also cannot help but evoke that garden out of which humanity, and the poet himself, has been expelled, Eden:

> a frieze of dogwood
> fence of forsythia
> of rose-purple iris
> an enchanted hedge
> outthrust of swords
> green as they be
> forbid flesh entry.

(But of course, a Johnson poem is rarely unequivocal: the garden of Eden is here fused with the magically briar-encrusted castle in which the sleeping Snow White—in Disney's version, no less—is imprisoned.)

The grounds and grasses of *The Shrubberies* evoke again and again the sexual freedoms of 1970s San Francisco: "foliate atriums / green allow pubis / cleft spine's base...splash into life / ultimate root." The picnic—the archetypal American pastime, when one comes upon a shaped landscape—brings to mind the liberatory play of an earlier era:

> at Satyr's campground
> Rainbow's saturnalia
> offering scapegoat
> capering round firepit

Johnson here recalls his membership in the "Rainbow Motorcycle Club." Picnics and campouts were frequently held; much leather was worn, cigars were smoked, beer was drunk; nobody in the club actually owned a motorcycle. The "scapegoat" here might be the chosen figure in some game, but the inhuman logic of the virus would make that figure all too literal: "accelerated commune with beyond / scattered many buddies' ashes / all swept in waltz of death."

In the mid-'90s, Johnson finds himself still alive, still striving to pull moments of vision out of everyday experience, but always waiting for the chill of finality, Dickinson's "Zero at the bone":

> across dark stream
> of shooting stars
>
> supplicant cast fly
> another year alive

> belief, belief brief
> zero at white core

What is astonishing is the beauty of the wee verbal performances Johnson produces out of these diminished circumstances, the light dances of sound and image that flash across these mostly white pages:

> plum-branch galaxy
> hoarfrost dark grasses
>
> breath, sounding web
> thistle listen cloud
>
> moth quicken afire
> seed silver, mirage
>
> a wind mirror pond
> shine white hyacinth

Or—

> sun in the honeyhives
> combing order from time,
>
> light on light suffuse
> like liquid copper
>
> climbing in the dark
> ore heights Byzantine

Flood Editions, a new imprint out of Chicago, has produced a physically beautiful volume out of Johnson's minute densities; and the poet Peter O'Leary has done a lovely job of editing *The Shrubberies*, sticking conscientiously to Johnson's final request to "prune the shrubs," even as he wanted to include a wider selection of the "shaggy," overgrown manuscript that Johnson left behind.

This volume includes, in addition to the Shrubberies proper, three further short pieces, including the last poem Johnson wrote before his death. It is a compact, moving performance, hanging desperately on to the visionary even in the face of descending darkness:

> shambles this way
> antipodean being
> come full circle
> sparks in darkness
> lightning's eternal return
> flipped the ecliptic

I can't help seeing a parallel between the curve of Johnson's career and that of his most idiosyncratic mentor, Louis Zukofsky. When Zukofsky completed *"A"*, among the longest of the great modernist poems, he immediately turned to *80 Flowers*, a sequence of eighty-one stringently formal, densely referential poems about—yes—flowers. Zukofsky was taking in sail, narrowing the compass of his work, and turning his eyes from the broad expanse of history to the minute greeneries that surrounded him (in this case, the potted plants his wife Celia nurtured all around the house).

80 Flowers is a beautiful but daunting read, yielding more to the ear than to the intellect on first (and twentieth) reading. Johnson's final horticultural vision in *The Shrubberies* is far more pellucid and immediately accessible than Zukofsky's, if no less aurally pleasurable. In conversation, Johnson once compared Swinburne's sonic texture to eating Turkish Delight—"but Zukofsky ... now that's chewing on a marrowbone." There is much "ear candy" to be found in *The Shrubberies*, but the aural lushness is continually countered by flashes of visionary incandescence, and by the touching melancholy of

Johnson's ruminative vision.

More Johnson is on the way. Last year Talisman House published *To Do As Adam Did*, a comprehensive selection of Johnson's poetry (edited by O'Leary). A number of Johnson's early texts, including the entire *Book of the Green Man*, are online at the Light and Dust Anthology website. Flood Editions will shortly reprint the long out-of-print *Radi Os*, Johnson's rewriting by excision of the first four books of Milton's *Paradise Lost*. Still waiting in the wings is *The Outworks*, a set of poems "surrounding" *ARK*.

It is all cause for rejoicing. In an age of dreary establishment verse, sneeringly cynical, broad-band ripostes against that establishment, and hyper-theoretical (and deathly serious) explorations of the workings of society and language, Johnson's work stands as an exemplary and wholly idiosyncratic demonstration of the joy that can still be found in poem-making and poem-reading. Even—as in the case of *The Shrubberies*—when that joy beckons from death's door.

Postmodern Poetry's Blue Period

Rachel Blau DuPlessis, *Blue Studios: Poetry and Its Cultural Work* (University of Alabama Press, 2006)

If one wanted to make such distinctions in the face of a collection that flaunts its own cross-generic status, one might begin by noting that Rachel Blau DuPlessis has distinguished herself in at least three separate sorts of writing. She is a celebrated academic literary scholar, author of *Writing Beyond the Ending: Narrative Strategies of Twentieth-Century Women Writers* (1985), *H.D.: The Career of that Struggle* (1986), and *Genders, Races, and Religious Cultures in Modern American Poetry* (2001). She is an innovative poet working in a post- or late modernist idiom, her most notable work surely the ongoing serial poem *Drafts*, three volumes of which are now in print: *Drafts 1–38, Toll* (2001), *Drafts: Drafts 39-57, Pledge, with Draft, Unnumbered: Précis* (2004), and *Torque: Drafts 58–76* (2007). And she has written a large number of pieces that she calls "essays," nonfictional critical and analytic writings that incorporate the formal and paratactic strategies of her poetry, and in which she never shies away from the first person. The frequently cited "For the Etruscans" (1979), something of a "breakthrough" text for DuPlessis, is the most readily recognized of these essays, a first collection of which was published in 1990 as *The Pink Guitar: Writing as Feminist Practice*. *Blue Studios*, then, is something of a sequel to *The Pink Guitar*, a new collection of essays: "essays" in the etymological sense of *forays, tries, attempts*—twelve attempts at definition and clarification that themselves resist the reader's defining or pigeonholing impulse.

The University of Alabama Press, in conjunction with its publication of *Blue Studios*, has reissued *The Pink Guitar* as well. Both books are included in the Press's "Modern and Contemporary Poetics" series, which in the ten years since its inception in 1998 has issued a striking variety of writing: not merely works of conventional literary criticism and scholarship, but also the collected occasional prose of such poets as Rosmarie Waldrop, Lorenzo Thomas, and

Jerome Rothenberg, anthologies of avant-garde southern and African American poetry, and a wide range of writing that falls under the rubric of "poetics"—poets' commentaries on their own practices and those practices' implications. Save for the anthology, there's a little bit of each of these genres in *Blue Studios*, grouped into four separate sections of three essays each: "Attitudes and Practices," three pieces on the genre of the essay itself and its place within DuPlessis's feminist writing practice; "Marble Paper," three essays in literary history (broadly defined); "Urrealism," three detailed readings of individual poets; and "Migrated Into," three reflections on the poetics and progress of *Drafts*.

"Blue Studio," DuPlessis explains at the outset, "is a pensive work site where a new world is hoped and an old can interrupt this hope. Thus it is a place of conflict and cross motives. *Blue Studio* is particularly a metaphor for working through negativity, an idea that threads through this book." "Blue" is at once the utopian poetic "azure" of Mallarmé and a dreary, defeated state of mind—"the blues." These sedimented cultural associations of the word, for DuPlessis, are imbricated with gender implications and with very personal associations:

> I began blue—as a *Blau*. This onomastic word offered me a talismanic color, and insofar as adults have such colors, it remains one. These essays negotiate a border between patriarchal culture and postpatriarchal culture—a utopian blueness in which the "blue" that is for "boys" crosses with my family name of origin.

While many academic writers allow themselves personal flourishes like this in the introductions to their books (or, more often, in the usually-skimmed prefaces), DuPlessis will maintain this mixture of registers throughout *Blue Studios*: writing in DuPlessis's essays is personal, always based in and referring back to DuPlessis's own experience of reading and thinking; it does not shy away from playfulness, in the form often of puns and etymological games, or from formal extravagances such as passages of lineated verse; and it maintains a theoretical sophistication and hard-nosed critical edge, a commitment both to complex formal analysis and ideological assessment. It's an all too rare combination to find in the writings of a literary scholar, and almost as rare to find in a writer identified as an "essayist."

The "informal" essay holds a tenuous place among academic discourses. Its exploratory nature, its refusal to structure itself around clear-cut theses, and its open embrace of the first person—the essayist's "voice"—have largely made it suspect within a literary studies discipline that spent much of the last century trying to establish itself on an "objective," quasi-scientific basis. The "essay" has acquired a pipe-and-brandy-snifter air of amateurish connoiseurism, while the "critical article" is the stock in trade of literary studies departments. Nonetheless, at least some literary critics and theorists, inspired at least in part by the dazzling examples of such writers as Roland Barthes, Susan Sontag, Walter Benjamin, Edward Said, and Theodor Adorno, continue to explore the essay form, even if the essay *per se* is still likely to be counted as less valuable, worth less in cultural capital than the analytic article. The academy's latest attempt to cordon off or to control the energies of the essay has been the establishment of "creative nonfiction" tracks within creative writing programs: here the essay has all too often been defined, disciplined, and tamed into a personal rumination or memoir. What is lost to literary studies when the essay is thus sequestered (or dismissed) is any clear sense of the critical, analytical power of the form, the way that the explicitly declared first person—as Thoreau writes in *Walden*, "We commonly do not remember that it is, after all, always the first person that is speaking"—can serve as a powerful fulcrum for untangling the relationships among social structures, personal histories, and aesthetic achievements.

The essay in DuPlessis's hands, however, is by no means as

straightforward a discourse as the essays of Henry David Thoreau, Cicero, or E. B. White. "*f*-words," for instance, "An Essay on the Essay," plays tentative, multidirectional games with the genre: the prose puns, backtracks, structures itself around a series of f-words enumerated at the end: "–fugitive, fissured, finding, effrontery, factor, fragmented, 'feminine,' foutisme, if ..." "Blue Studios: Gender Arcades," a response to a written query from younger poet Barbara Cole about the role of the "feminist poet," is presented in part as a straightforward letter ("Dear Barbara")—but it is also organized into separate, juxtaposed "arcades," breaks into several points into verse lines, and at one point includes a lengthy "brainstormed" list of what the term "feminist poet" might mean.

DuPlessis has done a good deal of thinking about the essay form and about her own particular variations upon it. The Introduction and first three chapters of *Blue Studios* ("Attitudes and Practices") present a number of explanations and manifesto-like justifications of her essay writing. "The post-patriarchal essay," she argues in the Introduction,

> offers a method of thought and an ethical attitude, not simply a style or a rhetorical choice. It is a method of the passionate, curious, multiple-vectored, personable, and invested discussion, as if a person thinking were simply talking in the studio of speculation, grief, and utopia. Essays can break the normalizing dichotomy between discursive and imaginative writing, between the analytic and the creative.

In "Reader, I married me: Becoming a Feminist Critic," an exhilarating autobiographical account of her own development as politically aware academic, DuPlessis describes the palimpsestic essay form she arrived at in "For the Etruscans" as "sensuous theorizing":

> If I choose to create desire, attention, loose ends, and an endless intersubjectivity between others as equals (undoing "the" binary),

then I am putting a little bit of utopian change into writing. The essay is antipatriarchal writing as a method of investigation and an instrument for change.

According to DuPlessis, the essay—or at least her own version thereof—is able to break both with the artificial impersonality of conventional academic writing, its spurious "objectivity," and with the self-centered monovocality implied in the MFA industry's unrelenting valorization of the personal "voice":

> The essay expressed community, even when apparently singular, and hence allows us to apprehend communitarian yearnings via what seems to be a private play of thought. Far from being exercises in narcissism, in gaining a personal voice, essays are practices in multiplicity, in polyvocality, in other opinions intercutting, in heterogeneous, faceted perspectives. In short, essays are not a way of "gaining a voice" but of losing one in the largeness of something else.

But is such writing as "For the Etruscans," and the other essays gathered in *The Pink Guitar* and *Blue Studios*, somehow inherently "feminine," in the sense that term has accrued from French feminist thought? While DuPlessis always identifies herself as a feminist, and presents her essays as part of a feminist counter-hegemonic practice—"For *Blue Studios* there is no way to be 'postfeminist'"—she is suspicious of the easy identification of her writing with an *écriture féminine*, a feminine writing whose formal heterodoxy is inherently liberating:

> The reason it has been blinding to call a certain rhetoric "feminine" is that it seems to credit our gender (speaking as Herself) with a style disruptive of hegemony. Yet it is not impossible (and can be seen, for example, in some of Charles Olson's essays) that this radical, rousing style can be coupled with ancient, patriarchal

gender tropes. Thus any call for the "feminine" in discourse is only interesting when crossed with a feminist, or otherwise liberatory, critical project; rhetorical choices are only part of a politics.

"'For the Etruscans' was widely taken to defend 'feminine language,'" DuPlessis reflects, but "what I actually said is that all rhetorical choice was situational and that nonhegemonic rhetorical strategies are often grasped by groups (women as 'ambiguously non-hegemonic') in need of oppositional statement."

This stance seems to me eminently reasonable, and it cuts to the heart of an issue that has bedevilled politically progressive writers and literary critics for three quarters of a century, from the so-called Brecht-Lúkacs debate down to the Language Poets: what is the relationship, that is, between "avant-garde" forms of writing (modernist and post-) and progressive politics? Or, as DuPlessis puts it, "How to calibrate the political meanings and contributions of creative practices?" Is there, as Julia Kristeva argues in *Revolution in Poetic Language*, an inherently counter-hegemonic charge to the disjunctive, nonlinear, or otherwise obdurately "difficult" texts of modernism, regardless of the political stance of the given writer? Or does such writing, as the examples of such reactionary modernists as Louis-Ferdinand Céline, Ezra Pound, T. S. Eliot, and Wyndham Lewis would suggest, especially lend itself to culturally or politically retrograde projects? The political implications of any particular specimen of modernist or postmodernist writing, DuPlessis argues, cannot be specified by an examination of the forms and rhetorics of that writing alone, but must be arrived at by studying the complex negotiations between the work's formal and rhetorical shape, its author's stated political stance, and the expectations of both a contemporaneous and a contemporary readership.

DuPlessis faults the poet Charles Olson (probably the first person to use the term "postmodernist" in a literary context) for "ancient, patriarchal gender tropes." Even more troubling, obviously, is the case of Ezra Pound, the anti-Semitic fascist whose work has wielded an incalculable influence on postmodern poetry, and on whom DuPlessis wrote her own doctoral dissertation. DuPlessis will not deny the importance of Pound's poetry for her own writing, and writes eloquently of the initial sense the Poundian "system" gives one of having engaged in a collective enterprise of knowledge and social correction:

> who among us of our generation who thinks at all of the literary has not been hailed into Pound's secretum (or perhaps to Olson's)— that sense that you were one of the cultural elite of knowers?.... you could do what needed to be done; you could articulate values without dialogue, in cadres, not in communities.

But Pound's particular modernism offered an ideological dead end: "Who has not been hailed into the band of knowers of Pound only to find that one was actually unable to read but only to parrot versions of Pound's unforgiving binaries?"

DuPlessis's long poem *Drafts* is quite consciously composed in *Canto*-length segments, and has a projected overall scale comparable to that of *The Cantos*: not so much in imitation, as in an act of "critical resistance":

> I wanted to make an alternative *Cantos*, a counter-*Cantos*. This is not so much a fantasy of Oedipal replacement (well, you tell me!) as it is a desire to place a counterweight inside culture and history, a poem with parallel ambition that comes to thoroughly different conclusions by different literary means.

DuPlessis may exaggerate the extent to which her project employs "different literary means" from Pound's—to my eye, there are strikingly *Cantos*-like moves and moments throughout *Drafts*— and her ambition to produce a "counter-*Cantos*" is an honorable but rather familiar one: William Carlos Williams's *Paterson*, Olson's *The Maximus Poems*, and Louis Zukofsky's *"A"* can all be read as self-consciously ideologically divergent responses to Pound's long poem. What is striking, however, is the very extent to which these works, along with DuPlessis's *Drafts*, parallel *The Cantos*, even as they work to overturn Pound's most basic ideological assumptions and assertions.

Which is perhaps to underscore the ideological *situationality* of rhetorical or poetic forms, that the non-linear, juxtapositional idioms pioneered by the modernists, while they may be to some degree subversive of established literary and cultural values, can work in either radical or reactionary directions—or in no particular direction at all—depending on the political stance of the writer under discussion. The true progressive heroes of the literary history DuPlessis gestures toward in *Blue Studios* are poets who quite consciously place their innovative practices in the service of subverting conventional political, social, and gender expectations. DuPlessis is perhaps at her best when considering the aesthetic achievements and ideological positioning of specific writers, as in her essays "Lorine Niedecker, the Anonymous: Gender, Class, Genre, and Resistances," which analyzes Niedecker's subversive reinvention of the nursery rhyme and the folk ballad, and "The Gendered Marvelous: Barbara Guest, Surrealism, and Feminist Reception," which considers Guest's poetic analysis and reinterpretation of the classic painter/model relationship, and of the surrealist movement in particular.

Most moving, by far, is DuPlessis's reading of George Oppen, "'Uncannily in the Open': In Light of Oppen." Oppen was a member of the short-lived "Objectivist" movement of the early 1930s, but would abandon poetry for a quarter century to devote himself to Leftist political organizing. When he returned to writing poems in the late 1950s, DuPlessis argues, he did so with no diminution of his egalitarian political commitments. Oppen was a major influence on DuPlessis's writing, in many ways her mentor (she has also edited an excellent *Selected Letters* of Oppen's [1990]), and her reading of how

Oppen's late work instantiates a new "epistemology" is striking indeed: "The strained, open, gnomic, and aphoristic line of his later poetry gives to him, but with a different ethics, a different epistemology, what surrealism gives to others: an investigatory tool to explore how the world may be put together differently by setting certain materials in combination."

This "different epistemology," in DuPlessis's account, is as well a utopian project, an ongoing existential and social critique of the world in which we live and an attempt at imagining a better one. I find DuPlessis's juxtaposition of Oppen's verse to Benjamin's *Arcades Project* and Adorno's *Aesthetic Theory* both apt and suggestive, though I hankered for more detailed readings of Oppen's own "gnomic and aphoristic" lines. While I think an extended reading of Oppen's poetry certainly bears out DuPlessis's description of his project, her all-too-brief analyses of passages from his poems—almost nods toward them—might leave a skeptical reader questioning whether her overall presentation of Oppen's work might not merely be a hopeful reconception of an exceedingly challenging and sometimes quite oblique body of writing.

DuPlessis's description of Oppen's poetics—"an investigatory tool to explore how the world may be put together differently by setting certain materials in juxtaposition"—may equally serve as a description of her own essayistic practice. It yields rich results in *Blue Studios*, whether she is considering the possibility of a feminist literary history ("Marble Paper: Toward a Feminist 'History of Poetry,'") in which Wordsworth's "The Solitary Reaper" is the primary object of analysis), or whether she is pondering the role of the "muse" figure in contemporary poetic manifestos by Allen Grossman and Charles Olson ("Manifests"). (Grossman's muse is the familiar female figure invoked throughout literary history, but the occluded "muse" behind Olson's "Projective Verse" manifesto is the scholar Frances Boldereff, whose enormous contribution to Olson's career has only recently begun to be acknowledged and explored.)

Once one has gotten used to the nonlinear progressions and exhilarating jumps of diction and register in DuPlessis's essays, more conventional academic writing is apt to seem somewhat wan and bloodless. "Propounding Modernist Maleness: How Pound Managed a Muse" is a fine contextualizing reading of Pound's "Portrait d'une Femme" in light of the poem's "model" Florence Farr, associate of and inspiration to George Bernard Shaw and William Butler Yeats and quintessential "New Woman," an excellent example of the illuminating work that has proceeded out of a reexamination of the specific contexts of modernist writing (tellingly, the essay was originally published in *Modernism/Modernity*, the "house organ" of the "new modernist studies")—but it is also the least engaging piece in *Blue Studios*, largely because of its conformity to the impersonal strictures of academic writing. I don't hear DuPlessis in this one, in short, and it's her voice (voices?)—witty, grave, chatty, winkingly stuffy, punning, layered, and inherently *polyvocal*—that makes this collection the stunning success it is.

Innovation's Explainer

Peter Quartermain, *Stubborn Poetries: Poetic Facticity and the Avant-Garde* (University of Alabama Press, 2013)

"The majority of the following poems," Wordworth wrote in the brief "Advertisement" prefacing the first (1798) edition of *Lyrical Ballads*, "are to be considered as experiments." Of course, one problem facing "experimental"—or "innovative," or "avant-garde"—writing is finding an audience prepared for its disruptions, willing to follow its deviations from the norm: his own readers, Wordsworth anticipated, "will perhaps frequently have to struggle with feelings of strangeness and aukwardness: they will look round for poetry, and will be induced to enquire by what species of courtesy these attempts can be permitted to assume that title."

Wordsworth felt compelled to become *Lyrical Ballads'* first explainer, in the lengthy Preface he wrote for the 1800 expanded reprint of the book; later, his collaborator Coleridge would devote a chapter of the 1817 *Biographia Literaria* to explaining what he and Wordsworth had been up to in a book which so decisively rejected the "gaudiness and inane phraseology" of the run-of-the-mill poetry of the day.

Like Wordsworth and Coleridge, twentieth-century avant-garde writers have been their own interpreters. Think of Stein's "Composition as Explanation," Joyce's endlessly detailed "schemata" of the structure of *Ulysses*, Pound's prose works and letters (which often read as commentaries on in-progress *Cantos*), and any number of essays and manifestos by Eliot, Mina Loy, David Jones, and so many others. But much of the heavy lifting required to mediate "difficult" texts for baffled readers has always been done by critics and scholars. A lot of what we understood of "high" modernism four decades ago was established in a series of brilliant volumes—on Pound, Joyce, Eliot, Wyndham Lewis, Beckett, etc.—by that irascible arch-Catholic Hugh Kenner. More recently, Marjorie Perloff, in what seems like a never-ending stream of books, essays, and reviews, has enthusiastically mapped and described a landscape of recondite new postwar poetries.

My own totemic figure among critics of twentieth- and twenty-first-century poetry has for a long time now been the English-born Canadian critic Peter Quartermain. When I was first grappling with the work of Louis Zukofsky and, like any good grad student, dutifully reading through what we call the "secondary literature," I noted two things: first, there hadn't been a hell of a lot written about Zukofsky; and second, a sizeable proportion of the very best essays on his work had been written by one Peter Quartermain. Quartermain's paper trail was not extensive: he had edited several volumes on twentieth-century American poets in that reference library staple, the *Dictionary of Literary Biography*, a labor which would not win one many laurels in the academy, but which was likely to help one toward a more comprehensive view of the field; and he had written a number of brilliant, jewel-like essays, sparkling with wit and interpretive insight and displaying the results of hard and discerning archival research.

Those essays were collected twenty years ago in *Disjunctive Poetics: From Gertrude Stein and Louis Zukofsky to Susan Howe* (Cambridge University Press, 1992). Since then Quartermain has become a major figure in the landscape of contemporary poetry. With the English poet Richard Caddel he edited *Other: British and Irish Poetry Since 1970* (Wesleyan University Press, 1999), and with Rachel Blau DuPlessis *The Objectivist Nexus: Essays in Cultural Poetics* (University of Alabama Press, 1999). For the past few years Quartermain has been hard at work on an edition of Robert Duncan's collected poems and plays, the first (massive) volume of which was published last year by the University of California Press. But *Stubborn Poetries*, perhaps surprisingly, is only the second full-length book to appear with Quartermain's name as author.

It's pointless to ask whether it's been worth the wait—and the twenty years since *Disjunctive Poetics* is, after all, a very long time: *Stubborn Poetries* is, simply put, a rich and marvellous collection, like its precursor a book that should be on the shelf of any serious reader of postwar poetry. Well—of a particular strain of postwar poetry, that is. Part of what Quartermain intends by "stubborn" poetry is *difficult*, obdurate poetry, writing in the modernist tradition that resists easy explication, blithe consumption. The canon celebrated here runs from Pound, Williams, Loy and Stein down through the Objectivists—Zukofsky, Lorine Niedecker, and George Oppen, along with their Northumbrian associate Basil Bunting—to Robert Creeley and various poets associated with the "Language" movement, Steve McCaffery, Lyn Hejinian, and Bruce Andrews. Along the way there are fascinating essays on a couple of outriders, Robin Blaser and the Englishman Richard Caddel, and a quartet of pieces on more general topics: bibliography in the age of the "distributed" book, the possiblity of a "proper" oral performance of a poem, the sort of "facts" that a poem deals with and indeed *makes*.

Quartermain is a splendid reader of Bunting, and "Basil Bunting: Poet of the North" both examines Bunting specifically as an outsider to the largely southern English tradition, and serves as an excellent introduction to Bunting's work for those who might be unfamiliar with it. Bunting's correspondent Zukofsky is well served here (in three essays), as is Lorine Niedecker (in two), who, as Quartermain demonstrates, is both a regionalist writer—a product of Wisconsin in the same way Bunting is a product of Northumberland—and a poet whose work strikes a deep, "universal" note, whose technique is as subtle and powerful as anyone around's.

It's good to read Quartermain on Blaser, who for too long has languished in the shadows of his friends Duncan and Jack Spicer. It's even better to read him on Caddel, a very fine poet who is almost entirely unknown in the United States, though I could have wished for less encomium and more interpretation—or at the very least quotation—of Caddel's work in the essay "'Writing on Air for Dear Life.'" Quartermain is capable of lapsing into a kind of clotted academese, especially when he's pursuing a tendentious tack, but for the most part his prose is delightfully wiry, precise and witty;

this is especially true when he's writing about poets whose work he obvious loves—Bunting, Niedecker—or when he's addressing an underappreciated countryman like Caddel.

What really makes *Stubborn Poetries* worth the price of admission, however, are Quartermain's close readings. Part of this is simply good old-fashioned formal analysis: Quartermain has a rare gift for taking apart the stress patterns of a set of lines and showing how they work, all the while paying careful attention to sequences of consonantal and vowel sounds. This is prosody pursued with a purpose. He's every bit as good at analyzing syntax, testing the possible combinations in which words might fit together. There's a kind of breathtaking *gravitas*, a combination of extreme concentration, painstaking attention, and sheer old-fashioned *patience* in his close readings.

This serves him best, perhaps paradoxically, when he's reading the ostensibly most "unreadable" of his texts, the obdurately reader-resistant works of McCaffery and Andrews. No, he doesn't tell us what they *mean*, and that's precisely the point; more usefully and more importantly, he shows us precisely how they simultaneously hold out the possibility of meaning (or meanings) and refuse any sort of semantic closure, the easy takeaway beloved of undergraduate paper-writers and book reviewers. Quartermain, for my money is the best reader of the illegible around.

I'm mildly frustrated, however, by his repeated insistence on their being some ultimately *political* charge in much of the "stubborn" poetry he so values, some utopian—or at the very least critical—potential inherent in the "difficult" text. It's an argument that's quite familiar from the Language poets, of course (though Geoffrey Hill has been caught making it lately, as well), and Quartermain gestures toward it in several of these essays. One variety is the old chesnut, familiar from any number of manifestos and essays produced in San Francisco and New York over the 1980s, of the difficult text making the reader a co-creator of meaning; this is surely true, I suppose, but I have yet to be convinced—even by Quartermain's honeyed and sinewy prose—that this is somehow necessarily *liberatory*. Quartermain, however, makes the argument for a utopian potential in experimental writing about as well and subtly as it can be made, and he rarely lets his ideological arguments get in the way of his nimble and ingenious close readings. I only wish he had allowed more space for what I'd nominate as the most utopian and liberatory affect of all—that of sheer readerly *pleasure*. Bruce Andrews's amazing and sometimes repellent *Lip Service*, in Quartermain's account, seems about as pleasant as a root canal: painful but good for you in the long run. It's really much more fun than that—honest!—if one can muster the necessary irony and *sang-froid* to tackle its jagged sexual and ideological *aiguilles*.

Quartermain is quite up-front about the occasionality of these pieces, and there's really no overarching argument tying the essays of *Stubborn Poetries* into a single foreseen curve. And that's just fine: this is a collection of celebrations and smart readings—readings in which "smart" very often edges over into "brilliant"—by one of the most intelligent and sensitive readers of poetry of our day, one of the finest sets of ears (backed by one of the most learned and inquisitive minds) of our moment. Yes—it was worth the wait.

The Book of Oz

Ronald Johnson, *ARK*, edited by Peter O'Leary (Flood Editions, 2013)

Ronald Johnson was the canonical age—thirty-five, "nel mezzo del cammin di nostra vita"—when he began his long poem in 1970. If *The Book of the Green Man* (1967) was his English book, and *Valley of the Many-Colored Grasses* (1969) his exploration of a visionary "American scene," then the poem he began under the unpronounceable title of "Wor(l)ds" would be Johnson's Book of Oz. He had left the grey prairies of his native Kansas and settled in the rainbow capital of San Francisco, where he moved between the company of avant-garde poets and that of leather-chapped bikers (or wannabe bikers). To pay the bills, he cooked, catered, and tended bar. On the side, he wrote literate, lyrical, calorie-insouciant cookbooks, hoping for the breakthrough volume that would catapult him to celebrity with James Beard and M. F. K. Fisher. That celebrity never came, though *The American Table* (1984), full of solid recipes and diverting anecdote, ought to find a place as one of the minor classics of its genres.

The long poem *ARK*—for Johnson's friend and sometimes bulldog Guy Davenport managed to argue him out of the awkward "Wor(l)ds" —occupied Johnson through the Seventies and Eighties, much less time than Pound, Williams, Zukofsky, or Olson had devoted to their own long poems. *The Cantos, Paterson, "A"*, and *The Maximus Poems*— all of them save *"A"* unfinished—are the uncomfortable precursors to *ARK*; but Johnson dodged what he saw as the "risks and shipwrecks" of his forebears through a couple of neat tricks. First of all, he would only attempt a poem *that could be finished*: *ARK*'s 99-section structure seems modest beside the sprawl of Pound's or Olson's vast texts, but that strictly delimited section-count, after all, let Johnson know precisely where he was at any point in the poem, and how far he had left to go. Secondly, this would be a poem *without* history: none of this "tale of the tribe" or "schoolbook for princes" business. *ARK* would be subject neither to conceptual derailing by the shocks of current events (see *The Pisan Cantos*), nor infinitely prolonged by the process of discovering new material, as in the later stretches of *Maximus*.

In one sense *ARK*, as thoroughly late-modernist as can be imagined in its prosody, its indeterminacy of meaning, and its radical parataxis, is a *science fiction* poem. Or perhaps an inverse science fiction poem. Science fiction at its best (when it's not just another genre—adventure, romance, what have you—sexed up with technology), through the estrangement-effects of imagined futures, imagined technologies, imagined social and biological relations, aims to cast a light upon the mundane world in which its readers all live. In *ARK*, Johnson aims to re-enchant our world, to make us aware of the wonder and fantasy inherent in the natural processes of which we are all both participant and product.

The sun rises at the beginning of the poem, BEAM 1—"Over the rim / body of earth   rays exit sun / rest to full velocity eastward pinwheeled in a sparrow's / eye"—and this miracle, light moving at almost 200,000 miles a second, is figured as "186,282 cooped up angels tall as appletrees." *Light*, and all of its ramifications, are at the heart of *ARK*. The SF writers of the "New Wave" might have taken *entropy* as their master trope during the Sixties and Seventies, but for Johnson the primary scientific reality is that our world is precisely not the closed system to which the Second Law of Thermodynamics applies: that the sun is continuously pouring energy into the biosphere, energy which transforms itself into heat, movement, structure: grasses, trees, sparrows, the human brain—a labyrinth of flesh "Convoluted of sun and dust," "the artificer of reality"—and the human eye, a "sphere of waters and tissue" which "may be said to be sun in other form": "After a long time of light, there began to be eyes, and light began looking with itself."

Johnson lays out most of his basic structures of wide-eyed wonderment in the thirty-three sections of *The Foundations*, appropriately enough. His overall metaphor for the poem as a whole is architectural: thirty-three "Foundations," each of them designated

"Beams"; thirty-three "Spires"; and thirty-three "Ramparts," called "Arches." (The practical implications of this scheme—how do you put "ramparts" on top of "beams"? and where's the *roof?*—don't much concern him.) After the conceptual groundwork of *The Foundations*, the second two-thirds of the poem is opened up to whatever catches Johnson's fancy: epitaphs for Louis Zukofsky and Robert Duncan, celebrations of the Bicentennial, bursts of song collaged out of Thoreau's journals, Van Gogh's letters, stacks of Protestant hymnals. Johnson pursues his work at a pitch of sustained glee and playful high spirits: he works through the permutations of anagrams and puns; he riffs on both high culture and low (many passages were drafted, I gather, in front of the television); he tries out variations of the concrete poetry in which he was so invested in the Sixties; he writes his way through the alphabet (ARK 55, *The ABC Spire*); he recasts *The Wizard of Oz* into lines that run the chromatic ROYGBIV notes of the rainbow:

> emerald, the front porch swing
> down yellowbrick road
> sun orange beyond the barn
> – Tornado Rose –
> beings stept forth in geode amethyst,
> nor atom blue of dust lost
> (ARK 64, *Rungs III, The Lilac Tree*)

Of course, there's no indigo in this six-line rainbow—but neither is there in the six-stripe LGBT Pride rainbow flag. (And the rainbow, one notes, is in French *arc-en-ciel*. Puns on "ark" are more or less ubiquitous in Johnson's poem, from the "Arches" of the Ramparts to the catalogue of animals entering Noah's vessel in ARK 83, *Arches XVII, The Ramp*.)

The pitch of wonder, and the variety of invention, flag somewhat in the Ramparts, each of whose thirty-three sections consists of eighteen three-line stanzas. At times one wonders if Johnson isn't simply losing focus on his project; certainly the tone shifts at times, as the chill atmosphere of San Francisco in the era of AIDS begins to infect even this most high-spirited poet. (One of Johnson's last published pieces, the as yet uncollected broadside *Blocks to Be Arranged in a Pyramid: In Memoriam AIDS*, confronts the epidemic head-on.) But the poem's ninety-ninth section concludes in a burst of star-reaching optimism, presenting the human being, this node of the branched energies of the sun, looking upward (with a nod to the Kansas state motto, "through difficulties, to the stars") to a stellar future:

> Origins great aorta
> leaved from the wrist up, but
> yet to attain the skies
>
> all arranged a rainbow midair,
> *ad astra per aspera*
> countdown for Lift Off
> ***

Johnson was publishing bits and pieces of "Wor(l)ds" through the 1970s, and the first book installment of his long poem—*ARK: The Foundations*, published in 1980 by Jack Shoemaker's North Point Press—was an auspicious beginning indeed. The slim, unpaginated, airy volume carried glowing blurbs from Hugh Kenner, Buckminster Fuller, Thom Gunn, and Guy Davenport, who was by that time by far Johnson's most vocal supporter. Charles Simic selected the next installment of the poem—*ARK 50: Spires 34–50*—for the National Poetry Series in 1984, and it was duly published by the emphatically mainstream E. P. Dutton, who must have been a trifle bewildered by what they were getting into. After the clean design and spacious typography of *The Foundations*, *ARK 50* came across alas as a rather dowdy book. A number of illustrations had popped up in *The Foundations* (including Leonard's ubiquitous Vitruvian Man, which

Johnson would later rightly remove); *ARK 50*'s center-justified poems were punctuated by a series of visionary architectural drawings by Johnson's friend Gordon Baldwin. They're reproduced a bit too small to be entirely effective, but they give the volume something of a sci-fi feel, which is I suppose entirely appropriate.

And after that came something of a hiatus. Further Spires would appear occasionally in periodicals, and for a while Johnson was sending out little bundles of Ramparts, carefully photocopied and stapled from his own typescripts, but it took a good long time—doubtless a dark time for Johnson: the worst days of the AIDS crisis in San Francisco, his own increasing financial difficulties, his retreat from Oz back to Kansas, where he spent his last years, his first bout with brain cancer—before any more of *ARK* would see publication in book form. The poem had been completed over half a decade (Johnson finished it on New Year's Eve, 1990) before Gus Blaisdell's Living Batch Press in Albuquerque would issue it complete in a single volume.

The 1996 Living Batch *ARK* was more than welcome for longtime readers of Johnson and for those merely *ARK*-curious, but it was a flawed blessing. Overall design was nothing to write home about, if not actively repulsive. But gutters in the prose passages are far too narrow, and the general trim size seems somewhat cramped, a trifle more compact than necessary. (I've often felt that as well about the University of California edition of Zukofsky's *"A"*.) More importantly, as Johnson's literary executor and editor Peter O'Leary has pointed out, the book is littered with typographical errors (some of them Johnson's characteristic misspellings, some of them introduced during typesetting); spacing and leading have been handled eccentrically; and a number of lines of verse and textual ornaments (even, in one case, an entire page!) have just plain dropped out.

O'Leary has been more than assiduous in managing Johnson's legacy. In the years since the poet's death in 1997, he has edited a career-spanning selection of his poetry, *To Do As Adam Did* (Talisman

House, 2000); has "pruned" and shaped *The Shrubberies* (Flood Editions, 2001), the baggy manuscript of short horticultural poems Johnson left in not-quite-edited form at his death; and has overseen a welcome new resetting of *Radi Os*, the revision-by-excision of the first four books of *Paradise Lost* that Johnson first published in 1977 (Sand Dollar Press; new edition Flood Editions, 2005)—the book that launched a thousand "erasure poetics" projects.

But *ARK* itself—Johnson's greatest achievement, and clearly the central edifice (to borrow his own architectural metaphor) of his writing—was already long out of print when Joel Bettridge and Eric Murphy Selinger published their grand cornucopia of Johnsoniana, *Ronald Johnson: Life and Works* (National Poetry Foundation, 2008). A sad spectacle: a 600-page, lovingly-prepared compendium of critical and biographical essays, interviews, and bibliographical data on a poet whose most important work was fetching upward of $200 on the rare book market, when it could be found at all. It's frankly been a long wait for the Flood Editions *ARK*, but to have the poem back in print, back in one's hands, is in itself a joy.

It's as a physical object that the new *ARK* first impresses one—a solid, substantial book, the title embossed in black on its almost-white-but-only-just-grey board cover, its title, author and publisher running down the spine in severe, sans-serif capitals: "ARK / RONALD JOHNSON / FLOOD" (a neat biblical pun, that juxtaposition of "ark" and "flood"; in Elysium, Johnson nods approval). After the black endpapers, the interior is as severe and unadorned as the cover: the typeface is starkly sans-serif (and rather small), the Os perfect circles. "Poems plain / as Presbyterian pews," Johnson extols in ARK 49, *Masthead*, but one can't help noting that his is also a poem of dazzling color, labyrinthine wordplay, not-at-all-Puritan lubriciousness: I guess illuminated capitals and ligatures are out of the question, but would just a *bit* of typographical dazzle be too much to ask? More importantly, these middle-aged eyes find it more than a little difficult to distinguish roman from italic in this typeface.

ARK's designer, Quemadura (that's the poet Jeff Clark), has become the go-to guy for contemporary alt-poetry, designing scores of covers and entire books for Ahsahta, FSG, and other publishers. He is to poetry books of the new millennium what the English firm Hipgnosis was to album covers in the 1970s. Don't get me wrong: for the most part I love Hipgnosis covers, and I like Quemadura's clean, abstract designs very much indeed, most of the time. But there's something almost too *pure* about the design of the Flood *ARK*.[1] I'll need to get used to it, at the very least. One worries, however, that in twenty years' time the book's design and typography may seem not timeless, but a characteristic product of millennials' nostalgia for postwar modernist design—all those white walls and fake Le Corbusier recliners one encounters in Manhattan apartments these days.

The typos have been cleaned up: the "caraytid" on the poem's second page has rightly become a "caryatid" (though Johnson's Orpheus still consistently seeks his own charmingly misspelled "Euridice"); the missing lines have been restored. Best of all, there are now page numbers, unobtrusive but terribly handy. My only remaining quibble, perhaps, is with the vertical spacing (the "leading," as typographers call it). Johnson himself worked back and forth between single and double carriage returns on his Selectric in producing his drafts, aiming for various effects. *ARK: The Foundations* and *ARK 50* tried with some success to reproduce those effects, but in the Living Batch *ARK* something has gone terribly wrong with the leading: it is a mare's nest, and quite unattractive indeed. I appreciate the challenge O'Leary faced in dealing with this issue: the Living Batch *ARK* is after all his copy text for the Flood edition, but the former's spacing can be reconciled neither with earlier volumes, nor with Johnson's typescripts. In the end, in order to "achieve greater legibility"—to create as *readable* a poem as possible—O'Leary has simply cut the

---

1. Literally. Those of us who do our morning reading in the company of coffee and tobacco are already cursing the brown smudges cropping up on the book's formerly pristine boards.

problem's Gordian Knot and adopted a uniform spacing throughout. While typographical issues are largely professional mysteries to me, I think I understand the decision. Which doesn't stop me from regretting it. At the very least the passages Johnson arranges *as prose* should have been set a trifle closer than they are.

But you know what that complaint is?: a quibble. We have *ARK* in print once again, in a more than handsome, reliably-edited volume. We can once again hold and read the whole of Johnson's ecstatic, moody, virtuosic, and just downright *loopy* vision, a divine—and mundane, and solar, and even interstellar—comedy for the space age and beyond. Rejoice!, reader, as you prepare to let Johnson "chorus us Homo Sapiens / in a major key!"

2. ESSAYS

Susan Howe's Hauntologies

In 1995, during the heady early days of the Kabbalah craze in the US, the New York record label Tzadik released a twenty-three-minute CD entitled *Zohar*, after the Kabbalistic "book of splendors," and credited to the "Mystic Fugu Orchestra." The music, one assumed, was a field recording from some Eastern European ghetto—it was hard to tell, given the utter absence of credits or liner notes (save for a long German quotation from Gershom Scholem)—and was obviously remastered from early twentieth-century 78 recordings (maybe even wax cylinders), for only through a haze of scratches, pops, and hisses could one hear Rav Yechida intoning what must be Kabbalistic chants over Rav Tzizit's spare harmonium. It is an eerie record, disinterring ghosts of a lost *Yiddishkayt*, gesturing toward a mystical tradition with continuities back to the Middle Ages, perhaps to antiquity. It is also a forgery. Rav Tzizit is John Zorn, the New York avant-jazz saxophonist and composer, and Rav Yechida is Yamantaka Eye, vocalist of the Japanese noise-punk band the Boredoms and frequent collaborator with Zorn on such projects as Naked City and Painkiller. The Mystic Fugu Orchestra's *Zohar* is musical hauntology, *avant la lettre*.

Susan Howe's long poem *A Bibliography of the King's Book; or, Eikon Basilike* was first published in 1989. It is a kind of palimpsestic ghost story, a spectral overwriting of a series of texts relating to the 1649 trial, execution, and afterlife of King Charles I: the *Eikon Basilike* ("The Image of the King") itself, a ghost-written (or flatly pseudonymous) series of meditations and prayers supposedly written by the King in his captivity; Milton's *Eikonoklastes*, a fiery response to the *Eikon Basilike* commissioned by Parliament, exposing (among other things) its author's plagiarisms; and Edward Almack's 1898 *A Bibliography of the King's Book; or, Eikon Basilike*, a bibliographical survey which is simultaneously an attempt to establish the "true" royal authorship of the *Eikon Basilike*. Howe's *Bibliography* is dominated by ghosts—the ghost of Charles I, whose last public word on the scaffold was "Remember"; the ghost of Hamlet's father, who famously speaks that same word to his son; other Shakespearean revenants, including the ghosts of Julius Caesar, Banquo, and Richard II; and the ghost, finally, of textual and historical authority itself. The prose introduction to Howe's *Bibliography* is appropriately titled "Making the Ghost Walk About Again and Again."

In its evocations of *Hamlet*, especially, Howe's poem seems oddly proleptic of a text that would be published four years later, Jacques Derrida's *Specters of Marx: The State of the Debt, the Work of Mourning, and the New International*. *Specters of Marx* was based on a pair of lectures delivered at the University of California, Riverside, as part of the conference "Whither Marxism? Global Crises in International Perspective"—a conference responding to the fall of the Berlin Wall in 1989 and the subsequent implosion of the Soviet Union, and specifically to Francis Fukuyama's triumphalist neo-Hegelian *The End of History and the Last Man* (1992)—and Derrida's book was to say the least a long- and eagerly awaited statement: at long last an explicit accounting of the relationship between deconstruction and Marxism.

I'm not so interested in Derrida's overall argument, his assertion that deconstruction has always operated "*in the tradition* of a certain Marxism, in a certain *spirit of Marxism*"—I agree with Terry Eagleton that a "New International" "without organization, without ontology, without method, without apparatus" is to any true Marxism much as non-alcoholic beer is to the real thing—as in *Specters of Marx*'s key neologism "hauntology." The term is in French a near homophone to "ontology"; it is, according to Derrida, a "logic of haunting" "which would not be merely larger and more powerful than an ontology or a thinking of Being.... It would harbor within itself, but like circumscribed places or particular effects, eschatology and teleology themselves. It would *comprehend* them, but incomprehensibly." Hauntology, as spectral logic or logic of haunting, describes the sense in which Marx himself, and utopian revolutionary hopes more generally, persist after the much-vaunted "end of history" (as described by Fukuyama—history ends, that is, when it reaches its *telos* in a world-wide late capitalist liberal democracy), but persist *spectrally*, both absent and present, uncannily eluding the categories of Western metaphysics.

The ghost appears in the first line of *The Communist Manifesto*—"A specter is haunting Europe—the specter of communism"—and Derrida is at pains to trace the surprisingly frequent appearance of specters, ghosts, vampires, and other uncanny revenants throughout Marx's texts. In counterpoint to these Marxian specters, Derrida places *Hamlet*, in particular the appearances of the ghost of Hamlet's father and Hamlet's own line, "The time is out of joint." The conjunction of these spectral figures, in a time "out of joint," leads Derrida to his formulation "hauntology." "Hauntology," like so many of Derrida's nonce words—"phallogocentrism," "différance," etc.—is a subtle, perhaps over-subtle instrument of analysis. And ultimately I'm less interested in Derrida's own deployment of the term than in the word's afterlife. "Hauntology," that is, has been taken up and deployed within pop music criticism, and in ways that correspond interestingly to Howe's project in *A Bibliography of the King's Book*.

In its most vulgar form, "hauntology" has been used to refer to any music that sounds "spooky," much as the popular lexicon deploys "deconstruct" when it simply means "analyze." More specifically, however, "hauntology" refers to a genre of popular music which relies heavily on sampling and quotation, which makes a "ghostly" music out of "'found' sounds, old television themes, soundtracks for public information film, allusions and debt to *musique concrète*" (this according to Bethan Cole). It is a music of nostalgia, indeed—nostalgia particularly for the sounds of 1960s and 1970s, the theremin whines of *Doctor Who* and the sound effects produced by the BBC Radiophonic Workshop—but it's as it were a "nostalgia for the future," for what inhabitants of previous decades imagined their future would sound like.

These things are hard to trace—especially for someone like me who isn't an obsessive reader of contemporary music criticism, much of which takes place on the rapidly expanding blogosphere—but the first print usage of "hauntology" in reference to pop music seems to be in Simon Reynolds's November 2006 profile of the English record label Ghost Box Music, published in *The Wire*. (Indeed, the pop music discourse on "hauntology" seems very often to use the word "ghost" as a jumping-off point; there was much talk of hauntology at the twenty-fifth anniversary re-release of David Byrne and Brian Eno's 1981 *My Life in the Bush of Ghosts* album—which some have taken as a foundational moment of the genre.) For Reynolds, the music issued by Ghost Box is "eldritch electronica." "Raiding vintage soundtracks and collections of incidental music," Reynolds writes, Ghost Box founder Julian House "leaves some snippets recognizable as orchestral playing but processes others to the point where they resemble ectoplasm or some supernatural luminescence out of an H.P. Lovecraft story."

I'd like to think the parallels between this description and the "ghostly" poetics of *A Bibliography of the King's Book* are obvious. Most clearly, the sampling techniques of contemporary musical production are precisely analogous to the quotational poetics Howe inherits from the earlier modernist works of Pound, Eliot, Olson, and others, and more generally from collage aesthetics such as that of Kurt Schwitters. (While quotation in classical compositions has been around as long as classical music itself, sampling in popular music didn't really take hold until the early 1980s, a clear instance of an latent artistic technique awaiting the technological developments that would make its full emergence possible—one might compare Adorno's argument about "original instruments" performances of Bach.) And Howe's quotational practice is not in the manner of Pound's or Eliot—snippets of previous texts, arranged as indices to their original sources—but resembles the "remixed," "smeared," or "processed" passages in a Ghost Box release: the documents quoted in *A Bibliography* are presented in tiny, often agrammatical shards, mixed together, overprinted, wrested even from the horizontal alignment of their original printing. They become a chorus of ghost voices, through which the poet herself, an Ariadne figure, must seek to trace a "thread" of coherence among the

"Driest facts / of bibliography": "I am a seeker / of water-marks / in the Antiquity / The Sovereign stile / in another stile / Left scattered in disguise."

In the wake of Simon Reynolds's dubbing this emergent subgenre of music "hauntology"—without, it seems, having bothered to work his way through *Specters of Marx* itself—other music critics and bloggers chimed in, complicating and subtilizing the concept in quite interesting ways. As the blogger K-Punk (Mark Fisher), points out, in reference to Hamlet's "The time is out of joint," "It is this sense of *temporal disjuncture* that is crucial to hauntology. Hauntology isn't about the return of the past, but about the fact that the origin was already spectral. We live in a time when the past is present, and the present is saturated with the past. Hauntology emerges as a crucial— cultural and political—alternative both to linear history and to postmodernism's permanent revival." What hauntology foregrounds, then, is the originary spectrality of the "original." Or, as Howe puts it in *A Bibliography*, "The absent center is the ghost of a king"— not the king himself, executed on January 30, 1649, but the king as the ghostly effect of a series of textual traces, from contemporary accounts of his trial and death, through the "ghost-written" *Eikon Basilike* and Milton's *Eikonoklastes*, down to the past century's bibliographies, which seek to pin down and "establish" texts which are no more to be captured than whiffs of ectoplasm. The "king"—the *arché*, the origin—is always already a "ghost."

Paradoxically perhaps, the critical discourse on hauntology, as writing about *music*, is cast in terms almost exclusively of *textuality*. Music is traditionally classified among the "performing arts," after all, and until fairly recently the default definition of "musical interpretation" was a performance of a work, not a bit of writing or talking about it. But hauntology, as a musical genre, is a music which is purely *produced*, rather than in any sense *performed*. And not coincidentally, the discourse of hauntology has arisen as the polar opposite of what in pop music circles has come to be derisively called "rockism"—the fetishization, that is, of "authenticity" in popular music: the rockist is he who automatically prefers punk to disco, Bruce Springsteen to Mariah Carey, The Strokes to M.I.A.; as one friend of mine puts it, rockism is to valorize "musicians who play *real instruments*." Rockism is the valorization, precisely, of *performance* over *production*.

The history of pop music is of course one of successive attempts to return to some "authentic," original image or performance: in the mid-'70s, Jerry Garcia of the Grateful Dead was recording acoustic bluegrass albums; the punk movement of the later '70s, with its DIY ethos, was explicitly an attempt to recover a more "authentic" rock energy in the face of disco and arena rock; more recently, such bands as Nirvana, The Strokes, The Hives, and The White Stripes have been hailed as returns to the "roots" of pop music. Perhaps the largest-scale such recovery moment in American music, at least, was the "folk revival" of the 1960s. The source-text of that movement was the six-LP *Anthology of American Folk Music* compiled by the polymathic mystic, archivist, and experimental filmmaker Harry Smith in 1952. The *Anthology* provided the young fogies of the late 1950s and early '60s an enormous treasure-chest of tunes and songs recorded in the 1920s and early '30s—folk, blues, gospel, cajun, etc.—upon which to draw, to be newly performed, adapted, and embellished. As the singer-songwriter Dave Van Ronk commented, the "*Anthology* was our bible. We all knew every word of every song on it, including the ones we hated."

In *Invisible Republic*, his book on Bob Dylan's *Basement Tapes*, Greil Marcus recounts how the *Anthology of American Folk Music* gave musicians—Dylan especially—a window into an America almost forgotten in the era of postwar economic prosperity and cultural conservatism, what Marcus calls "the old, weird America." But it is telling that when he describes Dylan and the Band's use of the *Anthology* in making *The Basement Tapes*, Marcus resorts to a hauntological metaphor:

What they took out of the air were ghosts—and it's an obvious thing to say. For thirty years people have listened to the basement tapes as palavers with a community of ghosts—or even, in certain moments, as the palavers of a community of ghosts. Their presence is undeniable; to most it is also an abstraction, at best a vague tourism of specters from a foreign country.

These "ghosts," Marcus goes on to argue, were not abstractions, but a "community" of "native sons and daughters" gathered together on Smith's *Anthology*.

But if Dylan, Van Ronk, Joan Baez and the hosts of other new folkies going to the *Anthology* for material thought they were tapping into some "authentic," originary slice of Americana, they were mistaken. As the blogger Richard Crary points out, "One of the important things to remember about the *Anthology of American Folk Music*, emphasized by Harry Smith but often overlooked, is that these were intended to be *commercial* recordings." Unlike much of the other music released on Moses Asch's Folkways label, the cuts on the *Anthology* came not from *in situ* recording sessions but from Smith's own vast collection of commercially released 78s. "The musicians may have been playing songs that had been around seemingly forever," Crary continues, "but these were not field recordings, these were *performances* recorded for release by record labels." In short, the *Anthology* was an broad-ranging compilation of commercially distributed regional American popular music, 1927–1932—but by no means a musicologically "authentic" representation of some indigenous culture.

Moreover, a listener's sense of these performances' "authenticity" is precisely a function of their technology by which the performances have been reproduced: the shellac record, with its tightly compressed sound and its inevitable high "noise" ratio. Commenting on the experience of listening to mythical bluesman Robert Johnson through the noisy medium of ancient 78s, K-Punk (Mark Fisher) makes a salient point about the "presence" of the past, about authenticity, rockism, and hauntology: "All that needs to be added to this is the idea that the 'mythologized deep south' arises *from* the 'layers of fizz, crackle, hiss, white noise'; there is no presence except mythologically, no myth without a recording surface which both refers to a (lost) presence and blocks us from attaining it." Compare, if you will, Moran Lee "Dock" Boggs's late 1920s recordings on the *Anthology* with his mid-'60s folk revival disks: the voice, the banjo technique are practically identical almost four decades apart, but it is the "recording surface," the distanced sound and the hiss and crackle that renders the earlier versions of songs both recognizably "authentic" and simultaneously spectral. In contrast, his clean and well-mic'd 1960s recordings sound like the performances of a folk revivalist.

"Rockism," K-Punk continues, "could be defined as the quest to eliminate surface noise, to 'return' to a presence which, needless to say, was never there in the first place; hauntology"—and here I take it he means as much the discourse of hauntology as the musical genre—"is a coming to terms with the permanence of our (dis)possession, the inevitability of dyschronia." For the rockist, the highest praise that can be given a studio recording is to compare it favorably with the band's live act, and rockism's quest for presence finds its apotheosis in the "live" recording, ideally free of after-the-fact overdubs and other cosmetic corrections: the "Support Live Music" bumper stickers bespeak not merely a fondness for seeing that musicians remain fed and sheltered, but a fetishization of *presence*, as instantiated in actual real-time *performance*.

Howe's *Bibliography of the King's Book or, Eikon Basilike* is also deeply interested in performance, but performance theatrical rather than musical. The poem is shot through with references to the theater, from a lengthy quotation from Sir Thomas More's unfinished *History of Kind Richard the Third*, to references to "Tragicum Theatrum Actorum," "dramatis personae," and "the stage of history"; Charles's execution is repeatedly referred to as "Tragedy." In drama, of course, "players" are not musicians but actors, and their speaking of particular lines and sentences always bears the stigma of theatrical performance: that the words spoken originate not from the speaker, but from the dramatic "part." Charles I is a spectral king largely owing to the difficulty of confidently attributing to him the words he is assigned. Milton's assault on the *Eikon Basilike*, for instance, makes much of the fact that the "King's Book" presents, as an authentic prayer by Charles, a speech lifted from Sir Philip Sidney's *Arcadia*. On the scaffold, Bishop Juxon tells the king that "There is but one Stage more, this Stage is turbulent and troublesome, it is a short one.... It will carry you from Earth to Heaven"—but is this "stage" the platform erected at the Banqueting House at Whitehall for Charles's execution, a stage on a journey, or a stage in a playhouse? And is Charles's last word to Juxon—"Remember"—an injunction to memory, or is it a quotation from *Hamlet* ("Adieu, adieu, adieu! remember me," says the ghost of Hamlet's father)? Charles was, after all, a devoted reader of Shakespeare, as Milton notes; was he *quoting* his dying word?

In the theater, performance is always interpretive or secondary, always mediated by playtext; and for Howe, history itself is fundamentally mediated by *text*, by the technologies of writing and print with their inevitable statics, the inevitable "noise," in the sense of that which is not "signal." "Noise," however, is not merely decay, the temporal degradation of a once-pure signal, but an inevitable formal component of communication or performance itself. "Modernity," K-Punk writes, "was built upon 'technologies that made us all ghosts'"—the prosthetic technologies, I take it, of the printed page and the mass media—"and postmodernity could be defined as the succumbing of historical time to the spectral time of recording devices. Postmodernity screens out the spectrality, naturalizing the uncanniness of the recording apparatuses." Hauntology, by contrast, whether in the "spooky" recordings of Ghost Box Records or on the scattered, haunting and haunted pages of Howe's attempts to sweep together the unmatching shards of history, foregrounds the "noise" and the imperfections of our "recording devices," whether aural or textual, and thereby recovers the uncanniness of history itself, the ultimate irrecoverability of a founding presence which was never there in the first place. "The absent center is the ghost of a king."

THE "HALF-FABULOUS FIELD-DITCHER": RUSKIN, POUND, GEOFFREY HILL

The public careers of the two close contemporaries J. H. Prynne (born 1936) and Geoffrey Hill (1932) might furnish an illuminating study in the sociology of late modernist poetry. As we enter the second decade of the new millennium, each of the two men is widely held up by American poets and academics as the most important English poet writing—but rarely by the same poets and academics. Prynne's career has been a study in public reticence and the dogged pursuit of ever more recondite experimental modes; his reputation has spread by word of mouth, as it were, and has been nourished by the almost mystical regard in which his writing is held by a coterie of very devoted readers (some of them his former students). Hill, on the other hand, has followed well-trodden career paths to his now almost assured canonical status: a first at Cambridge, followed by a quarter-century teaching at the University of Leeds and briefer stints at Emmanuel College, Cambridge (as Fellow) and at Boston University (as University Professor); a long series of books from major trade and university presses (Penguin, Houghton Mifflin, Oxford University Press, Yale University); and finally, the Oxford Professorship of Poetry in 2010.

Prynne's poetry has been disseminated—aside from his first (now disavowed) collection—by "little" presses, usually in the form of small print-run pamphlets (later collected in the imposing mass of his *Poems*, issued in successively expanded editions in 1982, 1999, and 2005). His works are eagerly awaited by a small but vocal readership, praised and debated on the internet and the blogosphere: but they have nothing like the exposure of Hill's collections, which receive front-page, full-length reviews in the major literary weeklies and notices in the big newspapers. What is striking, however, is that these two poets—the one (Prynne) enveloped in an air of hieratic Mallarméan mystery, the other (Hill) touted as the "finest British poet of our time" and "England's best hope for the Nobel Prize"—are both discussed more often than not precisely in terms of their *difficulty*.

That readerly "difficulty," I would argue, while it takes very different forms in Prynne's and in Hill's works, locates both men squarely within a modernist tradition. As I said at the outset, they are both late modernist poets, and while their works draw upon different aspects of the various revolutions in literary language and form pioneered in the early decades of the twentieth century, the very obduracy of their poetry testifies to the fact that literary modernism has yet to be assimilated to literary culture as a whole: that the revolutions begun by Pound, Stein, Williams, Eliot, Loy, and so forth remain a stumbling-block to reviewers and readers for whom the psychological and formal transparency of the Victorian and post-Victorian novel still stands as a measuring stick for literary achievement.

From a hundred years' distance, however, it is sometimes easy to forget the degree to which the modernists drew upon the Victorian culture that they so often vociferously rejected. While we can readily see the techniques of Dickens, Thackeray, and George Eliot repeated in today's bestselling "literary" novelists, it's a more complicated undertaking to trace the influence of the great Victorian cultural critics in the "high" modernist poets and those who have followed them.

* * *

Geoffrey Hill made his early reputation with a poetics of traditional form, of dense syntactic compression, and of formidable cross-grained cultural reference. If Hill's poetry has become less metrically strict, more earthily demotic, and less formally and syntactically costive through much the second half of his career—roughly, that is, from his move to the United States in 1988 to his present retirement in Cambridge—his work remains as densely referential, as forbiddingly intertextual as ever. He may sing the very personal praises of antidepressants in *Speech! Speech!* (2000) or indulge in an abrasive "*eat shit*" in *The Triumph of Love* (1998), but he remains a late modernist "quoting" poet in the direct line of Eliot and Pound, a poet whose work continuously evokes a wide range of historical and literary allusion.

By my reckoning, the body of Hill's poetry contains a half-dozen or fewer overt citations of the Victorian art critic John Ruskin (1819–1900). This count, however, belies the importance of Ruskin's social and aesthetic thought, and of Ruskin's general stance as a cultural critic, to Hill's own memorializing project. In many ways, Hill is a late Ruskinian, but a Ruskinian whose Ruskin stands in a crucial relationship to the thought of a poet whose own Ruskinism was largely unconscious: Ezra Pound. It would be going too far to say that Hill's Ruskin is in some way mediated through Pound; Pound, however, stands as a crucial Ruskinian precursor in Hill's meditations on the responsibility of the poet, and of the civic weight assumed by the artist in making art—meditations which find some of their most profound sources in Ruskin's own thought.

Ruskin, once an almost oppressively dominant figure on the Victorian cultural landscape, is these days less often read than invoked. He made his name in the middle decades of the nineteenth century and won an enormous readership with the five volumes of *Modern Painters* (1843–1860), the three volumes of *The Stones of Venice* (1851–1853), and the aesthetic manifesto *The Seven Lamps of Architecture* (1849). Ruskin looked at visual art and architectural ornament with an incomparably keen eye, and communicated his insights—in particular his sense, derived from his evangelical background, of the revelation of the divine in natural phenomena—in extraordinarily musical and evocative prose—"purple" passages that would be excerpted, anthologized, and admired throughout the last decades of the century.

From approximately 1860 onward, however—with the publication of the essays on political economy collected as *Unto This Last*—Ruskin's focus shifted from artistic and cultural criticism to a broader critique of existing social relations, an at-times-savage attack on Victorian progressivism, materialism, and laissez-faire economics.

While Ruskin continued to write art criticism and served as Oxford's Slade Professor of Art, talking about individual works of art became less important for him than a high-minded and quixotic attempt to set right the exploitative and soul-draining conditions of contemporary British society. His most notable efforts in this direction were the founding of the Guild of St. George in the 1870s, a number of books of political economy and social criticism, and *Fors Clavigera*, the series of monthly letters "to the Workmen and Labourers of Great Britain" he published regularly from 1871 to 1878 (and thereafter intermittently), which Guy Davenport has called a "a kind of Victorian prose *Cantos*" (and which might be profitably considered as a proto-blog).

By the time of his death in 1900, after a series of mental breakdowns and a decade of uncommunicative dementia, Ruskin had become a cultural institution, an inescapable presence in anglophone thought and letters. Hundreds of thousands of copies of his books were in print, and a "Library Edition" of his writings, which would run to thirty-nine massive volumes, was in preparation. If contemporary artists found him less than relevant, in part due to his lack of sympathy for Impressionism (exemplified by his infamous 1878 attack on Whistler), some still remembered his championing of Turner and his early support of the Pre-Raphaelites. Ruskin's ethical teachings were a primary influence on fin-de-siècle British socialism; members of the first British Labour Party to gain seats in Parliament in 1906 cited *Unto This Last* more often than *Das Kapital* as an influence upon their political views. And if the aestheticism of Pater, Whistler, and Wilde took elements of Ruskin's aesthetic teachings in a direction he would have found repugnant, his socio-aesthetic principles had been vigorously promulgated, in a popular and distinctly socialist form, by William Morris and his Arts and Crafts movement.

The young Ezra Pound, invested as he is in Whistlerian notions of artistic autonomy, has rather little directly to say about Ruskin, and what he has to say ranges from ambiguous to dismissive. In "*Yeux

Glauques," the sixth section of *Hugh Selwyn Mauberley* (1920), Pound sets the stage for a consideration of the early reception of the Pre-Raphaelites by noting that

> Gladstone was still respected,
> When John Ruskin produced
> "Kings Treasuries"; Swinburne
> And Rossetti still abused.

"Of Kings' Treasuries" is the first lecture of Ruskin's *Sesame and Lilies*, published in 1865 and his single best-selling book. While the syntax of this quatrain might initially imply that Pound is placing Ruskin in the same camp as the Liberal Prime Minister William Gladstone (whom Pound despised), a closer examination of "Of Kings' Treasuries"—a full-throated exhortation to cherish the cultural heritage preserved in books, along with a virtuoso demonstration of what seventy-five years later would come to be called "close reading"— and a consideration of Ruskin's role in promoting Pre-Raphaelite art suggest that he occupies a rather more positive space in the stanza's balancing of "blasts" and "blesses." Eight years later, however, in a brief essay on urban planning, Pound is rather more dismissive of Ruskin's social and technological conservatism: "Ruskin was well-meaning but a goose. The remedy for machines is not pastoral retrogression. The remedy for the locomotive belching soft-coal smoke is not the stage coach, but the electric locomotive..."

Ruskin is largely absent from Pound's social and critical vocabulary: he has no place among such luminaries as Confucius, A. R. Orage (editor of the *New Age*), or the Social Credit theorist Major Clifford Douglas. But this is because, paradoxically, Ruskinian principles are so pervasive that they have become the very premises of Pound's thought, accepted but unrecognized. There is an absolute congruence between Ruskin's statement, in his Inaugural Lecture as Slade Professor at Oxford (1870), that "The art of any country *is the exponent of its social and political virtues....* The art, or general productive and formative energy, of any country, is an exact exponent of its ethical life" and Pound's suggestion in *Guide to Kulchur* (1938) that "that finer and future critics of art will be able to tell from the quality of a painting the degree of tolerance or intolerance of usury extant in the age and milieu that produced it." What the two men share, that is, is a sense of "culture" as an "organic" totality in which aesthetic productions reflect social relations, in which the general health of a society can be gauged by a close analysis of its artworks, and in which the health of the arts depends upon the health of the society as a whole.

This sense of the organic dependence of artistic style upon social conditions, as Kenneth Clark points out, is absent before the nineteenth century. It first emerges in the architectural criticism of A. W. Pugin (1812–1852), but it finds its most eloquent, and incomparably most influential, exponent in Ruskin. If the Aestheticists made a great splash in the last decades of the century by insisting upon the absolute autonomy of the arts, they did so not merely because they were reacting against a vulgar Victorian moralizing, but because they were swimming against the current—or reversing the polarities—of a more sophisticated organicist conception of culture that had become widely diffused and deeply embedded in contemporary critical and social thought. (This is one of the great insights of Graham Hough's splendid *The Last Romantics*.)

It is this organicist conception of culture that Pound, after his early flirtation with aestheticism, returns to and embraces—without recognizing it as Ruskin's. Ruskin becomes the unacknowledged model for Pound's conception of the man of letters as culture-hero, as cultural warrior striving to clear a space for the production of healthy arts by reforming the ills of society. Artists, as Pound famously claims, are the "antennae of the race," and poets in particular are responsible for a kind of linguistic hygiene, a policing of the instruments of social interaction. They cannot fall into mere aestheticism or simple self-expression, but must constantly strive to cut through the cant of public discourse, holding up examples of more rational and humane ethical relations than those exemplified in society as it now stands.

The precise doctrines shared by Ruskin and Pound—while both men execrate usury and hanker for authoritarian, paternalist systems of government, the specific details of their social programs are radically different—are rather less important than their shared sense of the writer's task as an agent of cultural hygiene, as an active force for the renovation of society, its regrounding upon more sturdy economic and, ultimately, ethical foundations. When Ruskin uses his platform as Slade Professor of Art to exhort his undergraduates that "The England who is to be mistress of half the earth, cannot remain herself a heap of cinders, trampled by contending and miserable crowds," his stance is essentially identical to Pound's in the Preface to *Guide to Kulchur*, where he announces that "It is my intention in this booklet to COMMIT myself on as many points as possible.... Given my freedom, I may be a fool to use it, but I wd. be a cad not to."

Hill is one of the few English poets emerging in midcentury who have taken Pound's work seriously. His work, unlike that of the poets of the "Movement," has never shied away from the readerly challenges and cultural referentiality associated with "high" modernism. Indeed, in addition to its Poundian textures of dense referentiality, in recent years Hill's work has assumed an insistent rhetoric of *laus et vituperatio* (praise and execration) which places it in close company with Pound's. Hill encourages us to place his *laus et vituperatio* in the tradition of Lucian, of Dryden and Swift; but one of its most proximate sources, one might venture, are the "Blasts" and "Blesses" issued by Pound and Wydham Lewis in the first issue of *Blast* (1914).

It is precisely through the invocation of Ruskin that Hill is able, in his poetry, to make his most incisive engagement with the paradoxes of Pound's career. The references to Ruskin in Hill's earlier critical prose are rather few, but they have become far more more frequent over the past two decades. Ruskin's appearances in Hill's poetry have been rare but crucial. In section XXV of *Mercian Hymns* (1971), Hill "broods" on the eightieth letter of *Fors Clavigera*, in which Ruskin recounts his 1877 visit to a Worcestershire cottage in which two women are engaged in nail-making. It is a resonant moment in Ruskin's text (the very title of *Fors* can mean "Nail-bearing Fate"), and it perhaps unconsciously echoes the opening passage of Adam Smith's *Wealth of Nations*, which illustrates the division of labor through the similar example of pin-making. Ruskin celebrates the women's delicate efficiency at their task: "no dance of Muses on Parnassian mead in truer measure;—no sea fairies upon yellow sands more featly footed"; but he regrets not so much their straitened wages as the fact that "their forge-dress did not well set off their English beauty; nay, that the beauty itself was marred by the labour...." Hill, brooding on this episode in *Mercian Hymns*, "speak[s] in memory of my grandmother, whose childhood and prime womanhood were spent in the nailer's darg." "It is one thing to celebrate the 'quick forge,'" he writes, "another to cradle a face hare-lipped by the searing wire." Ruskin, Hill's passage seems to reflect rather acidly, has missed the point of the "nailer's darg": he has reduced or displaced the *human* costs of labor and production onto a purely *aesthetic* plane. But is of course a mark of how seriously Hill takes Ruskin that he is "brooding" over *Fors Clavigera* in the first place.

In later works, Hill will brood more deeply on the Ruskinian inheritance, particularly as it manifests itself in Pound's example. In his sequence "Pindarics (*after Cesare Pavese*)" Hill "reads through" and comments upon the anti-fascist Italian poet's diaries. Section 18 addresses a brief passage quoted from Pavese: "*Fundamentally the fine arts and letters did not suffer under fascism; cynically accepting the game as it was.*" "The nature it seems of that intelligence / is to be compromised," Hill writes: "P. (Ces) blamed Ruskin for the fascist state." (He alludes without quoting to another passage in Pavese's diaries: "The banality of totalitarian ideologies reflects the banality of the humanitarian theories that produced them. Tolstoi, Ruskin, Gandhi...") Hill clearly has little patience for such spongy thought:

"take your hook / and prune away among the vine-steads, clever man," he addresses Pavese, with no little sarcasm. But the conjunction of Ruskin's social thought and the "fascist state" brings in a middle term—the American poet most famously associated with Italian fascism, Ezra Pound. "Pound / was a Ruskinian," Hill writes,

> so it works out, so it
>
> fits and sits fair to being plausible;
> which is our métier.

Anyone with even a nodding acquaintance with Hill's fierce, almost disabling sense of rectitude, will recognize the savage irony in invoking "plausibility" as the poet's "métier." The work of the poet and poet-critic, as Hill interprets this inheritance from Pound, is not *plausibility* but *truth-telling*. To blame the fascist state on thinkers elements of whose thought might have been appropriated by fascism—as in the case of the French poet Charles Péguy, to whom Hill dedicates *The Mystery of the Charity of Charles Péguy* (1983)—is a failure of distinction, a failure of the poetic faculty itself.

But if Hill works to exonerate Ruskin from the charge of being a proto-fascist, he will waste no time on the fruitless task of exonerating Pound. The ultimate misdirection of Pound's ethical energies, how his desperate quest for a solution to the West's social crisis led him to outright, full-throated—and never really retracted—support of Mussolini's regime, is one of the most-repeated stories of twentieth-century literary history. Perhaps the most telling conjunction of Ruskin and Pound in Hill's poetry, section CXLVI of *The Triumph of Love*, addresses just this issue. The section ends with a moving paean to Ruskin:

> Ruskin's wedded
> incapacity, for which he has been scourged

> many times with derision, does not
> render his vision blind or his suffering
> impotent. Fellow-labouring master-
> servant of *Fors Clavigera*, to us he appears
> some half-fabulous field-ditcher who prised
> up, from a stone-wedged hedge-root, the lost
> amazing crown.

A couple of straightforward glosses are no doubt in order: "wedded incapacity" refers to Ruskin's famously unconsummated marriage with Effie Gray; and as "Master" of the Society of St. George, Ruskin regularly referred to himself in *Fors* as a "fellow-labourer" to the "Workmen and Labourers of Great Britain" to whom the letters were addressed.

Earlier in the section, Hill contrasts Ruskin to Pound on the basis of a verse from Deuteronomy:

> *Cursed be he that removeth his neighbour's mark*:
> Mosaic statute, to which Ruskin was steadfast.
> (If Pound had stood so, he might not have foundered.)

This passage (Deuteronomy 27.17) is a text—in the sense of a "text" around which a sermon revolves—which Hill takes as "implicit in [Ruskin's] major writings": "Cursed be he that remooueth his neighbours land-marke: and all the people shall say, Amen." Hill is certainly right in reading the defense of private property as a central Ruskinian theme. The basis of his distinction between Ruskin and Pound in this passage, however, lies not in any particular shared principle, but rather in the *steadfastness* that Ruskin displays, and which Pound fails to maintain. Both Pound's and Ruskin's ethical projects, in worldly eyes, must be reckoned failures: But Ruskin fails, not because he falters from his focus on remaking British society into something more humane and ethical, but because of the very unreachability of his goals and the fallibility of his instruments—the "fellow-laborers" who time and again prove unable to live up to his expectations, and his own too-highly wrought mental constitution, which eventually comes unstrung with the strain of his labors. Pound, in contrast, fails by letting his focus waver from a concern with the moral and technical weight of his own poetic technique, by allowing his attention to be consumed by the poisonous labyrinths of anti-monetarist and anti-Semitic conspiracy theories, allowing his imagination to be dazzled by "boss" figures such as Sigismundo Malatesta and Benito Mussolini.

Hill's own rehabilitation of Ruskin is by no means a matter of complete assent; most crucially, he finds he can no longer accept without qualification Ruskin's notion of "intrinsic value," once one of his own critical touchstones—a notion which I would tentatively identify as the "lost amazing crown" of the earlier passage. Hill's argument about intrinsic value, which surfaces in *The Enemy's Country* (1991, from lectures delivered in 1986) and occupies a central space in *Inventions of Value* (2008, mostly from lectures delivered between 1998 and 2001), is a subtle one, and his position changes over time. "Until recently," Hill writes in 2001, "I was an essentially an adherent of 'intrinsic value' as delineated by Ruskin. I am now much less sure of my position…" Ruskin himself, Hill notes, seems as convinced of the "intrinsic value" of some things as Thomas Hobbes is of the "inhaerent virtue" of the dead Sidney Godolphin to whom his *Leviathan* is dedicated; but that very dedication on Ruskin's part to the "intrinsicality" of value wavers in *Fors Clavigera* 37, when his never-precise definition of value seems almost to merge with the proto-labor-theory of Locke's *Second Treatise of Government*.

Hill's discussion of Ruskin in the lectures of *Inventions of Value* and his invocations of Ruskin in *The Triumph of Love* and "Pindarics (*for Cesare Pavese*)," then, play upon the *elegiac* force of Ruskin's invocations of "intrinsic value," an "unwobbling pivot" for socio-economic commentary that has proved to be a broken reed. In the face of Ruskin's failure, and even more so in the face of Pound's folly, Hill finds himself reflecting again upon the improbability of the poet's actually *influencing* society. "Still, I'm convinced," Hill writes in *The Triumph of Love*, "that shaping, / voicing, are types of civic action": the tenor of that poem as a whole, however, makes this assertion seem little more than whistling against the wind. And any such "civic action," in the midst of a culture gripped by an accelerating historical amnesia, is by necessity a rear-guard action, of memory and reminding, of what David Jones called "anamnesis." By the end of that long poem, Hill has come to concede that the poet's task is no more or less than to preserve a rigid fidelity to his own language, so that his works might serve as acts of witness and memorialization. And this, of course, has been the tendency of Hill's poetry all along, from the formal elegies and Holocaust poems of *For the Unfallen* (1959) and *King Log* (1968) right through the impassioned homages of *Without Title* (2006). It is surely a diminished conception of poetry's mission, especially in the light of the society-changing power that Ruskin and Pound attributed to letters; but it is a little better than the bleak view of poetry that closes *The Triumph of Love*: "a sad and angry consolation."

The "Net / (K)not—Work(s)" of Robert Sheppard's *Twentieth Century Blues*

Beginnings

Toward the very end of "A"-12, Louis Zukofsky adapts the opening invocation of the *Odyssey* to address his wife Celia: "Tell me of that man who got around / After sacred Troy fell.... / Tell us about it, my Light, / Start where you please." However much Homer's epic may be rooted in an oral tradition, the "telling" of Odysseus' story we encounter when we pick up a copy of the poem begins not at some semi-arbitrary moment of pleasure, but at a closely calculated—and later formally codified—*in medias res*. There is nothing to stop us, as readers of long works, from beginning our readings "where we please" (Derek Attridge has suggested that neophyte readers of *Ulysses* might as well start at the beginning of Chapter 4, "Mr Leopold Bloom ate with relish" etc.), but in the tradition of Western writing both novelists and poets have expended enormous energies crafting memorable and resonant beginnings for their works: The virtuosic sixteen-line sentence opening *Paradise Lost*, which ranges from the poem's subject ("man's first disobedience"), through the advent of Christ, the second Adam ("one greater man"), to the revelation of Torah to the "shepherd" Moses, to a gutsy assertion of Milton's own ambition to pursue "Things unattempted yet in prose or rhyme"; the first phrase of Pound's *Cantos*, "And then went down to the ship," which as it overlays an Old English diction on a fifteenth-century Latin translation of Homer's archaic Greek, superimposes the English conjunction *and* over Homer's first syllable—"*And*ra moi enneppe ..." (and significantly hearkens back to the neutral *and* by which the King James translators chose to render the polyvalent Hebrew conjunction *waw*); "A / round of fiddles playing Bach," the opening of Zukofsky's "A"-1, which binds into a historical ring the 1729 Leipzig premiere of the *St. Matthew Passion* and its 1928 New York performance.

Disseminations

The circumstances of publication and dissemination of many twentieth-century long poems, however, have made "starting at the beginning" problematic for the average reader. When Zukofsky received his copy of Pound's 1930 *A Draft of XXX Cantos*—a sumptuous limited edition; ordinary readers would have to wait till 1933 for a trade printing—he had only read a handful of the Cantos published thus far; he had begun his own long project, *"A"*, in 1928 with little idea of the overall shape of *The Cantos*, the work to which it would later be compared, and which he would be accused of aping. *"A"* itself was even more difficult of access for the average reader: the first movement to appear in print was "A"-7, published in 1931; since that movement is in part a telescoping of the themes of the first six movements, it was probably incomprehensible to most readers. The first six movements of *"A"* would only appear as a unit in the 1932 Zukofsky-edited *An "Objectivists" Anthology*, a book published in France, and which no doubt had little circulation in the United States. But just as modernist poets adapted to their own aesthetic ends the artisanal economies of the small presses and little magazines to which they were exiled by their exclusion from trade publishers and large circulation journals, by the latter half of the twentieth century poets such as Allen Fisher and Robert Duncan had begun to work principles of piecemeal dissemination into the formal structures of their serial poems.

Place / Passages

Notable in this regard are the English poet Fisher's multi-volume *Place* (1971–1980) and the American Duncan's sequences *Passages* and *Structures of Rime*. Duncan began dispersing poems of his *Structures of Rime* through *The Opening of the Field* (1960), and added to it in each of his collections through the end of his life, though in later collections it was somewhat displaced by poems from the sequence *Passages*, which Duncan described as "Passages of a poem larger than the book in which they appear." At one point, the two sequences overlap: "An Illustration, *Passages* 20 (Structure of Rime XXVI)"; and by the middle of *Ground Work: Before the War* (1984) Duncan had left off numbering the poems of *Passages*, inviting the reader thereby to trace his or her own path among them. Similarly, in the second volume of his large topographical poem *Place, Unpolished Mirrors* (1985), Fisher proposes six different orders of reading the work; Fisher has consistently maintained "that a reader can join the project at any point, becoming the 'loci of a point on a moving sphere.'"

Twentieth Century Blues

Between 1989 and 2000, English poet Robert Sheppard wrote *Twentieth Century Blues*, a 75-section work—or as *Twentieth Century Blues* 14, "Untitled," has it, a "net / (k)not work(s)"—that as of this writing (February 2007) is spread over four separate collections, *The Flashlight Sonata, Empty Diaries, The Lores*, and *Tin Pan Arcadia*, and a number of fugitive pamphlets and broadsides. *Twentieth Century Blues* is a searing exploration of twentieth-century history and subjectivity, and is as notable for its formal variousness—Sheppard deploys word-count and syllabic prosodies and a wide variety of stanza shapes—as for its thematic range. Equally compelling is Sheppard's thorough rethinking of the "serial poem" form. Inspired by the multiple reading paths offered in Fisher's *Place* and by Barrett Watten's theorization of formal refunctioning in Zukofsky's *"A"*, Sheppard constructs a serial poem that invites multidirectional, recursive readings, and which is traversed by various subsidiary and overlapping shorter sequences, or "threads." "We can all read the object, assemble, re-assemble it in our own way(s)," Sheppard writes. "This will, of course, be affected by our acquired knowledge, our perceptual schema, and by the means of the texts' availability, not an irrelevant question for the non-canonical poet, relying upon fugitive small presses. We all have to start reading with what we can get...."

Labyrinth; or, Maze

My own obsession, fueled by a similar labyrinth-obsession among some of the "high" modernists—Joyce's artist-figure is named after Daidalos, builder of the Cretan labyrinth; David Jones figures the trenches of the Western Front as labyrinths in *In Parenthesis*; Bunting writes of "Schoenberg's maze" in *Briggflatts*—is to seize upon the labyrinth as formal analogy for *Twentieth Century Blues*. A double analogy, thanks to a happy semantic slippage: The classic *labyrinth*, as found on cathedral floors and beloved of New Age spiritualists, is a unicursal contruction, guiding the viewer or walker through multiple turns to a single goal. An edifying spiritual exercise, perhaps, but of little use in containing a fierce Minotaur or preventing a prisoner from escaping. As instructive is the common usage of "labyrinth" as equivalent to the more modern *maze*, a construction characterized by multiple paths, choices, turnings—and occasionally, multiple entry and exit points. *Twentieth Century Blues* hovers between the labyrinth and the maze: there is a single, unicursal path through the project, authorized by the poet, but one is simultaneously tugged away from that path by the various "side-tracks" of the "strands" to which many of the poems belong, and which extend beyond *Twentieth Century Blues* itself. And even this unicursal path is characterized by maze-like repetition and recursiveness.

"Logos in Kimonos"

Let me be a bit more specific about this "recursiveness": Here is a poem from Sheppard's 1998 *Empty Diaries* entitled "Logos in Kimonos" (I was inclined at first to read this Greekly, like "Empedocles on Etna," but it becomes clear that Greek-looking words here are far more commonplace):

> The sky was sick metallic skin, genethetic
> meat loaf rotting over the hot city.

Poor kids still rode the Underground. Smart
Arses like me skated the neural Tanks,
clipping onto Personality Composites. My latest catch
was an Autoflesh case. My biomatic orgasm
flushed Yen in the cybernetic maelstrom, where
he'd picked me up on feel alone.
Information sickness iced me, pink fuses blowing,
melting subliminals in the cool jelly stolen
from the Tanks. Logos on kimonos flashed
fleshy machines. I'd MEAT and METAL lasered
on either tit and I could clip
ecstasy any time I liked. Flooded by
voices, not mine, in the Tanks: nostalgia
for human dust on the keyboard, ancient
meat messages flattened on the screen. When
I watch old movies I get sentimental
over robots, strutting like pillheads from a
bar at 5. CyberCunts fleshed on me
by some clipwrecked pilot with a scrimshaw
virus flutter my optic lashes to process
the orgasm I'll use to crash his
information-dead eyes. He's hard copy. Once
I've jellied my button, he'll jack me
like a deck, then roll off, a
dead man.
      The realisation that neither of
us is human makes my flesh creep.

This is a cyberpunk poem, almost a parody of William Gibson's 1984 novel *Neuromancer* (compare its opening sentence, "The sky above the port was the color of television, tuned to a dead channel"), spoken in the voice perhaps of Daryl Hannah's character Pris in Ridley Scott's *Blade Runner* (1982), a "basic pleasure model" with a homicidal streak. The poems of *Empty Diaries* present a moving picture of the sexual and political violences of the twentieth century, told for the most part (according to the book's back cover copy) "by a succession of female narrators, each one of whom 'knows' she is narrated by a man."

Recursions

One might of course read "Logos in Kimonos"—as I first did—in its context in *Empty Diaries*, a series of poems that cover, one for each year, the years 1901 to 1990. (In that context it seems rather out of order: it is "Empty Diary 2055," between 1987 and 1988.) But if one follows the sections of *Twentieth Century Blues* in numerical sequence, one encounters "Logos in Kimonos" as *Twentieth Century Blues* 16. Six sections later, one will read "Logos in Kimonos" as a section of *Empty Diaries* Part 4, which is *Twentieth Century Blues* 22; two sections after that, one reads the whole of *Empty Diaries* as *Twentieth Century Blues* 24. One has then read "Logos in Kimonos" three times (the same is true of *Empty Diaries* 1990, which is *Twentieth Century Blues* 19, as well as part of *Twentieth Century Blues* 22 and *Twentieth Century Blues* 24). The effect, one might argue, is analogous to traversing the same pathway in a maze on successive turns, or encountering the same painting or sculpture in different passes through a large and complexly organized museum, each time noting how the piece has been recontextualized by its presentation within a larger whole.

Turnings

But the maze of *Twentieth Century Blues* includes not merely recursive repetition, but side-paths, numbered "threads" reappearing as subtitles throughout the poems ("Bolt Holes," "I. M.," etc.). "Logos in Kimonos," as well as being "Empty Diary 2055," is "Duocatalysis 8," "History of Sensation 6," "Human Dust 1," and "Fucking

Time 2." The first "Fucking Time" poem, a series of responses to John Wilmot, Earl of Rochester, is *Twentieth Century Blues* 15. (The title is taken from Aubrey's life of Fr. Franciscus Linus, who erected a set of exquisite but phallic sun-dials in his garden "which were one night ... broken all to pieces by the earl of Rochester, lord Brockhurst, Fleetwood, Shepard, etc., comeing in from their revels. 'What!' said the earl of Rochester, 'doest thou stand here to ... time?' Dash they fell to worke.") The third is *Twentieth Century Blues* 25, "Flesh Mates on Dirty Errands." "Threads" such as "Fucking Time" offer the reader other options for reading order, and emphasize the "network"-like (or as Sheppard hazards, "rhizomatic") structuring of the work. Such "rhizomatic" form authorizes greater readerly choice, even compositional authority. We can read "Logos in Kimonos" in its order within *Twentieth Century Blues* (if we are conscientious, we read it thrice); or we can turn aside from *Twentieth Century Blues*' primary numerical ordering and follow—backward, forward—any of the "threads" to which it belongs, whether "Fucking Time," "Duocatalysis," "History of Sensation," or "Human Dust."

Shuffling / Flipping

Whichever path we choose when we reach Twentieth Century Blues 16, "Logos in Kimonos," is perforce shaped by the books we have at hand. "History of Sensation" 1, 3, and 4 are contained in Sheppard's 1993 volume *The Flashlight Sonata*; 2 is available only in a limited edition chapbook or broadside I have not seen; later sections are contained in *Tin Pan Arcadia*, the largest concentration of *Twentieth Century Blues* yet published. *Twentieth Century Blues* 63, "The End of the Twentieth Century: a text for readers and writers," an essay in poetics that is included in every one of the approximately *fifty-five* "strands" that traverse *Twentieth Century Blues*, has yet to appear in book form. Whichever path we take through Sheppard's "net / (k) not—work(s)," we must do a good deal of shuffling of books and flipping of pages. Indeed, *Twentieth Century Blues 74* is not a poem but a detailed index to the project as a whole, and Sheppard has produced as well an index to the work's "strands." This is a poetic sequence which, like the turnstile handout at some nightmarish Magic Kingdom, contains its own detailed and indispensible visitor's guide and map.

Tension

The conceptual, the *readerly* tension here—of which I think Sheppard is well aware—is that between the traditional linear, page-based presentation of the individual poems, and the spatial conception of the network as a whole. Can there be a *verbal* network, or a *verbal* labyrinth, given that poetry from Homer to Sheppard subsists as a pattern of sounds (phonemes) or marks (graphemes) moving forward and down the page in a single socially agreed-upon order? It is a tension analogous to that which Zukofsky identified in "A"-6: "*Can / The design / Of the fugue / Be transferred / To poetry?*" Not a rhetorical question.

Presentation

The ideal presentational form for *Twentieth Century Blues*, it seems to me, is a hypertextual one, a web-based environment where a reader could click on an icon at the corner of each poem in order to be taken to the next (or previous) section of *Twentieth Century Blues* or to the next (or previous) poem in each of the "strands" to which the immediate poem belongs. In some ways, Salt Press's forthcoming publication of a single-volume *Twentieth Century Blues*, like Reality Street's single-volume edition of Alan Fisher's *Place*, works to foreclose the combinatory possibilities offered by a hypertextual presentation (or, as Sheppard suggests in his Note to the volume, a "box publication" like that of Duchamp's *Box in a Valise*). Sheppard is well aware of this, and even as he is grateful to Salt for making possible a "collection of works intended as a network, but never a Work," he notes how a "codexical presentation" "raises questions of organization that the box and the hypertext evade." "In a sense," he writes, "this book is another strand (as any ordering a Reader makes within it is a strand), one which I hope will make the individual blues present as apart from, as well as a part of, the network."

Collection

As Sheppard explains in a note to the forthcoming Salt *Twentieth Century Blues*, this vast project is in essence a collecting and arranging of all the poems he wrote "between December 1989 and 2000," with the addition of a number of related texts dated from 1983 to 1989—a "kind of Collected Poems 1989–2000, with a Selected Poems 1983–1989 interpolated into it." The typical procedure for producing a "collected poems," of course, is simply to string together chronologically the contents of the author's previously published volumes, though Sheppard is by no means original in deviating from that practice: Laura (Riding) Jackson's 1938 *Collected Poems*, for instance, arranges her work achronologically under various thematic headings—"Poems of Mythical Occasion," etc.—and Marianne Moore's 1967 *Complete Poems* is not complete at all, but presents a closely culled and revised selection from her body of work. What is remarkable is how Sheppard has radically *refunctioned* his various works by arranging them within the network of *Twentieth Century Blues*, and by positioning them on the various threads that traverse and go beyond *Twentieth Century Blues* proper.

Service

All of this is in the service of an ethics of readerly authority about which one has heard much, from the theorists of the American

Language school in particular. I quote Sheppard again: "We can all read the object, assemble, re-assemble it in our own way(s)." In earlier critical statements such as "Propositions 1987" and "The Education of Desire," Sheppard had written of poetry's defamiliarizing effects as crucial to the education of readerly desires, to the fostering of a politically or socially critical consciousness. More recently, he has taken to reading the political ethics of his work as "less utopian, less the text opening horizons of possibility, Marcuse's Aesthetic Dimension glittering with its prefigurations" and more openly critical and "strategic: a denial of what we presently are…" "The aim, however," Sheppard writes, "has not changed: to activate the reader into participation, into relating differences, to sabotage perceptual schema, to educate desire, not to fulfill it in a merely entertaining emptying of energy. To create, above all, new continuities." Some of those continuities, some of those readerly options, will be necessarily occluded in the forthcoming Salt *Twentieth Century Blues* (Sheppard speaks of his attempt to create "a satisfying page-by-page read"): those occlusions, I think, will be outweighed by the pleasure of having this simultaneously densely woven and terminally "frayed" work between a single set of covers.

"I AM NOT AN OCCULTIST"

Esotericism, Literary History, and Autobiography in *The H.D. Book*

Charles Olson and Robert Duncan first met in in Berkeley in 1947, where the towering Melville scholar, out West to research a book on the Donner party, had looked up the younger poet on the strength of his *Medieval Scenes*. Their conversation on that occasion dwelt more on California history than on poetry, but over the next few years Olson increasingly came to see Duncan as a fellow-traveller in his own effort to forward the next "push" in American poetics. There is a rueful tone, then, to the monitory essay-letter "Against Wisdom as Such," which Olson published in 1954 in the inaugural issue of *Black Mountain Review*, a warning against the pitfalls of esoteric "wisdom" —gnosis, insight—arrived at from outside the poet. "I wanted even to say," Olson writes in an aside, explicitly withdrawn, "that San Francisco seems to have become an *école des Sages ou Mages* as ominous as Ojai, L. A."

Ojai, a Ventura County valley town, was perhaps best known in the early 1950s as the home of Jiddu Krishnamurti, who early in life had been groomed as something of a Theosophist "messiah"; Olson's reference thereto must have struck Duncan as a gentle poke at his own Theosophist upbringing. The sentence seems to have still rankled Duncan some seven years later, after his stint of teaching with Olson at Black Mountain College, and after the publication of Donald Allen's *The New American Poetry* had given shape to something literary historians would call "Black Mountain Poetry," for he quotes it in Part II of *The H. D. Book*, in a chapter dated 11 March, 1961. "There is something about looking behind things," Duncan retorts; "There is the fact that I am not an occultist or a mystic but a poet, a maker-up-of things."

The poet, one fears, protests too much, or quibbles over terminology: for as "Beginnings," the vast first section of *The H. D. Book*, a dazzling tour-de-force of scholarship, confession, and practical poetics, amply demonstrates, the terms "occultist," "mystic," and "poet" are consanguineous in Duncan's imagination; indeed, his own conception of the poet's calling is founded upon a reading of modernist literary history in which formal and stylistic innovation, the canonical hallmarks of modernism, are deeply bound up with the uncovering of esoteric knowledge. To be a "poet" of Duncan's stripe is fundamentally to interest oneself in what is "occult," hidden, or "mysterious": if Duncan rejects the terms "occultist" or "mystic," he does so not on the basis of the words' dictionary meaning, but of their connotations.

The H. D. Book begins as autobiography, retailing—as do so many spiritual autobiographies, both ortho- and heterodox—an experience of conversion or vocation. "It is some afternoon in May," Duncan writes, "twenty-five years ago as I write here—1935 or 1936—in a high school classroom. A young teacher is reading." What that teacher (Miss Keough) is reading is H. D.'s poem "Heat," first published in Ezra Pound's anthology *Some Imagist Poets* in 1915. And what that first reading—or rather, that first audition—constitutes for the sixteen-year-old Robert Symmes (Duncan's childhood name), listening in the classroom, is a calling, a "vocation." "Unconscious of the content that made for that imprint and awakened in me the sense of a self-revelation or life-revelation in the pursuit of Poetry, I was conscious only of my own excitement in the inspiration—the new breath in language—and of a vocation. Whatever my abilities, it was here that I had been called to work."

The narrative of conversion through a text is a basic *topos* in Western culture. Perhaps the most famous example is that of St. Augustine's *Confessions*, where the thirty-two-year-old Augustine, believing in the truth of the Christian revelation and convinced of his own sins, but still torn by the desires of the flesh, is walking in his garden in tearful internal debate; he hears the voice of a child: "*Tolle, lege, tolle, lege,*" it says—"take it and read, take it and read." Augustine seizes the nearest copy of scripture he can find—the Pauline epistles—and opens to just the passage that addresses his own plight: "Let us walk honestly, as in the day; not in rioting and drunkenness, not in chambering and wantonness, not in strife and envying. But put ye on the Lord Jesus Christ, and make not provision for the flesh, to fulfil the lusts thereof" (Romans 13.13–14). And his conversion is effected. In this case, a text already received as sacred speaks to the immediate spiritual situation of the its reader.

In other textual conversion narratives, a previously occult, unreadable text is made legible through the offices of an interpreter. The paradigmatic example is that of the Apostle Philip and the Ethiopian eunuch in Acts 8. Philip encounters the eunuch in his chariot, reading the prophet Isaiah: "He was led as a lamb to the slaughter, and like a lamb dumb before the shearer, so opened he not his mouth" (8.32, cf. Isaiah 53.7). "Understandest thou what thou readest?" asks Philip; "How can I," answers the eunuch, "except some man should guide me?" The apostle proceeds to open to him the occluded, typological meaning of the passage—it prefigures Christ, of course—and the eunuch is converted, forthwith initiated into this new fellowship by the rite of baptism.

One can multiply examples, both sacred and secular, of the vocation-through-text, up to the very present. I'm reminded of Guy Davenport's childhood encounter with Edgar Rice Burroughs's *Tarzan*, or the thirteen-year-old John Ruskin's present of Samuel Rogers's topographical poem *Italy*, with illustrations by J. M. W. Turner—a book, he would later recall in his autobiography *Praeterita*, which determined "the entire direction of my life's energies." But Ruskin's next sentence is crucial: "it is the error of thoughtless biographers to attribute to the accident which introduces some new phase of character, all the circumstances of character which gave the accident importance. The essential point to be noted, and accounted for, was that I could understand Turner's work, when I saw it;— not by what chance, or in what year, it was seen." In order for the reader/auditor to be *called* by the text, that is, he must be prepared to receive that call: Augustine through his years of scriptural study and spiritual struggle, the Ethiopian eunuch through his devotion to Hebrew scripture, the young Ruskin through his annual tours of the landscapes and private picture galleries of England. And Duncan, as the brilliantly unwinding layers of "Beginnings" will demonstrate, has been prepared to received H. D. and the whole discourse of poetic modernism—a very specific version of modernism, that is—precisely by his early immersion in the culture of Theosophy, astrology, and hidden spiritual wisdoms.

There are two threads I would want to trace here: on the one hand, there's the outline of modernist poetry, and of the poetic vocation, that Duncan delineates in Part I of *The H. D. Book*; and on the other, there is his manner of presentation, the way he unfolds the "secret history" of modernism in this strange, branching text. I will only gesture toward the latter, charging you to see for yourself—"*tolle, lege.*" Suffice it to say that these chapters cunningly intersperse Duncan's narrative of his conversion to poetry, his vocation, with what begins as a straightforward literary history of Imagism, the literary "movement" within which "Heat" was produced. But only begins, for immediately Duncan shifts his focus to aspects of modernism which the literary historians of his day were far less anxious to emphasize.

Led by Pound's own rhetoric in his various Imagist "manifestos," literary history takes the primary injunctions of the Imagist movement—as Duncan sums them up, "image, composition by musical phrase, and verbal economy" as a set of hygienic measures aimed at the otiose Georgian lyric, measures that could easily degenerate into the "Amygist" principles of "impressionism, *vers libre*, and everyday speech." But the roots of the modernist revolution are far more complex than a mere reaction against post-Victorian letters: they include Madam Blavatsky's Theosophy; the nineteenth-century traditions of automatic writing and mediumistic séances; the anthropological investigations in comparative religion of J. G. Frazer and Jessie Weston.

Imagism in particular, Duncan argues, when read within the context of the esoteric tradition evoked in Pound's *The Spirit of Romance*, is something far deeper than a tightening up of the poetic vocabulary. "An 'Image'" (capital I, in quotes), we recall from Pound's early Imagist manifesto "A Few Don'ts," "is that which presents an intellectual and emotional complex in an instant of time." Pound would have us read "complex" in "the technical sense employed by the newer psychologists": but what it suggests more immediately for Duncan is the psychology—the science of the *psyche*—of the Neo-Platonist Porphyry (which is who Duncan means when he writes of "Psellos"), or of Dante, or of the Troubadours, who might have evolved, out of "half memories of Hellenistic mysteries, a cult stricter, or more subtle, than that of the celibate ascetics, a cult for the purgation of the soul ..." "Complex," then, as Pound uses it, is according to Duncan

> a node involving not only the psyche, as that term used by modern psychologists, but the soul, as that term is used by esoteric schools. So too, the quotation marks and the capitalization, setting the word "Image" apart, carried for the knowing reader the sense that the word had a special meaning beyond the apparent. "Image" and "Intellect" in the framework of Gnostic and neo-Platonic doctrines that haunt Pound's cantos to the last are terms of a Reality that is cosmic and spiritual; they are terms of a visionary realism.

And from here in "Beginnings" Duncan is on fire, interweaving his account of his own awakening to poetry with that of a secret history of early modernism, a secret history, he notes, which has been wholly obscured by the critical and poetic hegemony of the mature, Christian T. S. Eliot. This is modernism not as formal disruption, nor as youthful reaction against enervated post-Victorian poetics, nor even as a disciplinary tightening-up of poetry in the face of an increasingly bureaucratized society; rather, Duncan's account is of a modernism which is above all else a resurgence of ancient, occluded wisdom. "I believe," Pound wrote in 1930, replying to Eliot's question "What does Mr. Pound believe," "that a light from Eleusis persisted throughout the middle ages and set beauty in the song of Provence and of Italy."

The historical accuracy of Pound's "light from Eleusis," the theory that elements of the Eleusinian Mysteries survived into the Middle Ages in southern Europe, decisively influencing the culture of courtly love, the growth of Provençal lyric, and thereby early modern European poetry in general—or what I prefer to call the "Da Vinci Code" theory of poetry—is not the issue. (For the record, Pound seems to have derived it for the most part from two long-discredited books, Gabriele Rossetti's *Il msitero dell' amor platonico del medio evo* [1840] and Joseph Péladan's *Le secret des troubadours* [1906].) What is interesting, in the context of Duncan's reading of modernism, and his call to poetry, is the structure of Pound's writing as an uncovering of esoteric knowledge. For Duncan, the "secret history" of modernism cannot be separated from modernist innovation; indeed, such innovation as the palimpsestic forms of H. D.'s novels and long poems and the ideogrammic structure of Pound's *Cantos* are precisely manifestations of the esoteric or occluded webs of spiritual knowledge that underwrite poetry as a human practice of making. In the deft and burgeoning weave of "Beginnings," Duncan traces a secret history and, through his autobiographical narration, inserts himself into an hitherto hidden order of poetry that is revealed by the high modernists, but which *contains* modernism itself.

THE MASTER OF SPEECH AND SPEECH ITSELF
NATHANIEL MACKEY'S "SEPTET FOR THE END OF TIME"

Nathaniel Mackey's "Septet for the End of Time"—published first as a chapbook by the Santa Cruz Boneset Press in 1983 and then collected in Mackey's first full-length volume *Eroding Witness* (University of Illinois Press, 1985)—immediately confronts its reader with the order of numerology, and beyond that with the order of speech itself, the saying that incarnates the numbers. Its three epigraphs provide three possible numerological entries into the eight poems: that of the Dogon elder Ogotemmêli (as transcribed by the French anthropologist Marcel Griaule); that of the Quran; and that of the *Pyramid Texts of Unas*. Others can be adduced: the seven stars, seven candlesticks, and seven seals of the Book of Revelation; the "septet" (*septuor*) of Mallarmé's "Sonnet en –yx," that multivalent constellation (Ursa Major, the Big Dipper, Charles's Wain) whose appearance is the fulcrum of revelation in an implacably motionless tombeau for the Western poetic tradition; and the *Quatuor pour la fin du temps* of the French composer Olivier Messiaen, whose resolutely personal musical vision was as rooted in the traditions of Roman Catholicism as Mackey's is in the cultural heritages of the African diaspora.

At some level, perhaps a level of number, the eight movements of Messiaen's unusual quartet (composed and premiered in a German prisoner-of-war camp, scored for piano, clarinet, violin, and cello) mirror the eight poems of Mackey's "Septet." But while Messiaen's spiritual universe is predicated upon the absolute presence of a Christian God, upon the strong assurance that the Apocalypse given St. John is available not only in the jagged rhythms and angelic textures of the quartet's music, but will be revealed to the believer "in the flesh," Mackey's is an eroding witness: the self can recognize its cultural, spiritual roots only as eroding traces in the works of others, and that recognizing self is in turn eroded, like the figure illustrating the cover of *Bedouin Hornbook* (the first-published installment of Mackey's ongoing fiction, *From a Broken Bottle Traces of Perfume Still*

Emanate), by the forces of history, distance, and time itself.

There are eight poems in the "Septet," and like a master musician Mackey is actively engaged in playing eight against seven. "'Seven,' said Ogotemméli, 'is the rank of the master of Speech; 1 + 7 = 8, the eighth rank is that of speech itself.'" The Quranic text Mackey quotes (sura 18, verse 22) identifies seven "sleepers": "Seven: Their dog was the eighth." The "Septet," then, is the representation of eight sleepers awakening and, by the act of announcing their awakening, entering the order of "Speech itself": each poem begins, "I wake up...," but these awakenings are not to the logic of daytime reality, but the surreal logic of dream, in which metamorphic images and shifting orders of discourse impose an identity, new for each poem, upon an "I" that bears only a vexed, oblique relationship to the monological "I" of the Western lyric tradition.

In some of the poems, the "I" takes on in part the voice of the poem's dedicatee: the saxophonist Pharoah Sanders in "Capricorn Rising," the Guyanan novelist Wilson Harris in "The Sleeping Rocks" (which echoes Mackey's "Song of the Andouboulou: 4"), the Brazilian singer Elis Regina in "Falso Brilhante," the painter Jess (Collins) in "The Phantom Light of All our Day," and Messiaen himself in "Winged Abyss," whose title alludes to "Abîme des oiseaux," the astonishing third movement (for solo clarinet) of the *Quatuor*. To some degree, Mackey is repeating Pound's gesture here, casting the poems' voices in that of "personae," masks though which the poet develops his own vision. But where Pound's personae follow Robert Browning's in their monological, personistic recreation of historical figures, Mackey's poems shift and erode under the reader's feet, mixing past and future, Western, Eastern, and African. "Dogon Eclipse," for instance, recounts the sage Ogotemméli's blinding in a hunting accident, only to tip the reader into one of Marcus Garvey's "erratic ships":

> A debt of bullets taken years before
> as I fall back blinded...Up-

> start sun I slip thru careful not to
> cross my legs and as my
>   gun misfires
> feel I've boarded one of Marcus'
> erratic ships, aborted Black Star Line,
>   prophetic
>   ark of unrest...
> Withered lid of an eroded "I,"
> Ogotemmêli overlooks the lit city
> outside [...]

The order of speech, then, is an order of the present, in which past and future are simultaneously present—not in a linear sense, or in the sense of Eliot's "order of monuments," but in a spiritual order of traces in which the temporal present is as much an eroding trace as the remembered past or the presciently known future. The speakers of these poems wake up again and again, not from dreams to waking "reality," but from dreams to dreams, from one order of language to another—from an order of music to that of its mythic equivalent, and back again, from an order of death to life-in-death and death-in-life.

What the "Septet" suggests is not that there is no reality outside of language ("il n'y a pas de hors-texte," as the young deconstructionists used to trumpet) but that the orders of reality—orders which are as much spiritual as they are historical—are embodied and embraced in the culturally structured orders of speech. While Mackey's speakers may desire like Stephen Dedalus to awaken from the "nightmare" of history, their repeated awakenings are a reiteration of the self's utter entanglement in the network of cultural traces that constitutes it.

The jazz great Pharoah Sanders, for instance, is represented as resisting the powerful force of the music that both works his liberation and locates him within a tradition of oppression, "a / thin bread of duress, / a / sea-weary drift of boatlifted / Haitians...":

>   I wake up mumbling, "I'm
>   not at the music's
>   mercy,"   think damned
>   if I'm not, but
>   keep the thought
>   to myself
>   ***
>   hungered by
>   its name, what of
>   it I refuse
>   forks an angel's tongue,
>   what of it I refuse awakes
>   the wide-eyed
>   stone

Olivier Messiaen's own voice comes through "Winged Abyss" both in its own interiority and as a pure manifestation of the musical order that so thoroughly pervades Mackey's work:

>   A war camp quartet for the end of time
>   heard with ears whose time has yet to
>   begin...
>   An unlikely music I hear makes a world
>   break
>   beyond its reach...
>
>   So I wake up handed a book
>   by an angel whose head has a rainbow
>   behind it.
>   I wake up holding a book announcing the
>   end of time.

As Mackey tells it, the birdsong of the "Quartet" announces not the end of the world, but the dissolution of a European conception of time and history, a conception whose death-knell is rung in the concentration camps of the Nazi Holocaust, geometrically intensified versions of the camp that gave rise to Messiaen's own apocalypse:

>   A lullaby of wings, under-
> neath whose auspices, obedient, asleep
>   with only one eye shut, not the
>   end of
> the world but a bird at whose feet I hear
>   time
>   dissolve ...

Messiaen's own vision, at once archaic and stridently modern, has distinct spiritual affinities with Mackey's:

>   I hear talk.
>   Out of touch
>   with the times, I wake up asking what
>   bird
>   would make so awkward a
>   sound

But while Messiaen's *Quatuor* celebrates a divinity and a revelation that constitute a real presence in the world, no matter how "awkward" to the ear, Mackey's "Septet" speaks over and over to the absolute contingency of the noumenal, its presence only in the "Broken music-footed / ghost" of memory and language.

The transcendence achieved through music is but another order of speech, of communication (witness the interpenetration of music and discourse in the prose narrative of *Bedouin Hornbook*); but that music, as in all of Mackey's work, represents the promise that the labor of dream and memory might lead one eventually out of the inferno of history, the "single catastrophe which keeps piling up wreckage upon wreckage and hurls it in front of [our] feet" (Walter Benjamin): in "Dogon Eclipse," Ogotemmêli

                                        Hears the drum the
    djinns beat to the sky, Tabele,
        beat, its rhythms waste
     us, weightless dream and
                            so ended
   search...

              All as though one's
     feet would find their way without
                                escort
            All as if by then I'd
                           been thru
Hell
    and back

3. 100 POEM-BOOKS

100 Poem-Books

Introduction

I think it's probably hard for millennials to imagine how "slow" the poetry world was back in the dark ages of the 1980s and the early 1990s. One got the news of new books, of readings, of new magazines and book series through actual print media—magazines, newsletters, mass mailings—or though word of mouth. From 1994 on, one might subscribe to the Buffalo Poetics List, which would fill your e-mail in-box with a daily deluge of announcements, notices of readings and publications, comments and commentary, and sometimes acrimonious flyting, both against literary and political figures outside of the List and among List members themselves.

The advent of the weblog opened up the scene exponentially. Anyone with access to a computer and an internet connection could start a blog, and could post whatever they wanted, as often or as rarely as they wanted. And as long as that blog was "public," anyone else could read it, and post comments on it, and link to it. Ron Silliman began his "Silliman's Blog" in August 2002 with a modest statement:

> Blogs have been around for awhile now, but to date I haven't seen a genuinely good one devoted to contemporary poetry, so it may prove that there is no audience for such an endeavor. But this project isn't about audience. The fact that the blog has the potential to carry forward the best elements of a journal and seems inherently prone to digressive, if not absolutely plotless, prose gives me hope that this form might prove amenable to critical thinking.

"Silliman's Blog" turned out to be a game changer, at least for me; Ron posted regularly and sometimes copiously, reviewing new books, returning to old favorites, thinking about the relationship of poetry as a formal, political, and social art to this new landscape in which poets' and critics' avenues of communication had suddenly entered what seemed a utopia of instantaneousness.

"Silliman's Blog" was by no means the first devoted primarily to poetry, but it was the first to enter my consciousness in a big way, and I suspect the same was true for many of the poets of my generation and the generation after. Over the next couple of years, poetry blogs sprang up like dandelions after a spring rain, and one found one's blogroll exploding. Some people used the form to post their own poems; others used it for relentless self-promotion, announcing their readings, books, and periodical publications on a regular basis; others confined themselves to commentary and musings. I found myself spending more and more of my time reading weblogs, following back-and-forth conversations, discovering new poets, poems, and books.

As usual, I was a late adopter of the form. When I began my blog "Culture Industry" in March 2005, I thought I saw in the blog medium a perfect twenty-first century analogue to John Ruskin's *Fors Clavigera*, the series of monthly "Letters to the Workmen and Labourers of Great Britain" (pamphlets, really) he issued between 1871 and 1884. The issues of *Fors* provided Ruskin a space to publish whatever he pleased; the pamphlets, available by subscription only, were printed to his specifications—he had no editor to answer to. He could write about a news item that had caught his attention; he could excoriate the moral state of the ruling classes; he could dwell on a work of art he loved; he could write serial installments of a biography of Sir Walter Scott; he could speculate about Theseus' haircut and its relation to the priestly tonsure; in short, he could do whatever he wanted.

Of course, if the blog could be a kind of open space for speculation, it could also be a public forum in which I could try to *hone* my writing and thinking—a kind of serial version of Theodor Adorno's aphoristic *Minima Moralia*. (My title "Culture Industry" was of course a nod to Adorno.) In the event, I didn't achieve either Ruskin's sprawling, free-range creativity or Adorno's deliberate and penetrating intensity; or at least I didn't achieve them very often, or very much to my satisfaction.

"Culture Industry" turned out to be a rather heterogeneous affair: part book notices, part diary, part working notebook. I posted an occasional poem; I announced a forthcoming or recent publication; I linked to a YouTube video I liked. But a significant portion of the writing I posted on the blog was actually substantial (at least in my own assessment). I gave it thought, care, and energy; it elicited useful responses.

Much of the poetry blogosphere's energy has ebbed in the last half-decade, as people's energies and attention have migrated to even more instantaneous social media—Facebook, Twitter, Instagram. I was taken aback a few years ago to read a young poet's comment on Facebook about "the old blogging days," as if the weblog were a quaint and archaic artifact of the past, like the Model T, 78-rpm records, and the handwritten letter. Yes, I suppose the half-decade of intensive blog-writing and back-and-forth blog exchanges are a thing of the past, and that's not really something to be mourned, but part of the way of the world. Hard thinking about and intensive discussion of poetry still takes place, just in other venues: electronic, print, and face-to-face. "Culture Industry" itself, while still out there, has become something of a rarely-updated random journal. But its archives—and those of "Silliman's Blog" and a host of others—are there to be looked over by anyone who's interested in what held poets' attention in the first decade of the millennium.

* * *

All of this as something of a long-winded introduction to the following notes on poetry books, originally posted on "Culture Industry" between January 2008 and March 2010. My immediate inspiration came from Jonathan Mayhew's wonderful blog "Bemsha Swing" (which takes its title from a Thelonious Monk composition). Mayhew is for my money one of the smartest readers around of poetry, in both Spanish and English. His blog posts tended to be short, intense, and incisive.

Mark Scroggins

In January 2008 Jonathan decided to read through and blog a hundred novels:

> I don't read much fiction, so I've decided to read a little more in those "dead hours" when I'm usually just randomly flipping through blogs and such, say 9:30 to 11 p.m. I'm reading 100 novels and blogging about them. It might take a year or two. My plan is to start somewhat randomly and, if I like a particular novel, read another by the same author. If I don't like it, I'll switch to another author. The blog tag "100 novels" will help me keep track of what I've read. Since it's a "stretching exercise" in some respects I'm not reading novels that I know I'll like in advance, or revisiting old favorites.

I was inspired, as I often am by Mayhew's gestures and ideas. (We share, I think, a kind of mild OCD.) What follows is my own response, a series of readings/impressions of a hundred volumes of poetry, with the blog tag "100 poem-books." These one hundred entries fall somewhere between the stools of brief review and rapidly sketched reading notes; they *try*—not always successfully—to avoid the condition of the blurb. (I'll admit that a couple of them along the way have been appropriated by publishers to serve precisely as blurbs for poets' further books.) I've left them largely as I initially wrote them, though I've expanded ampersands and some contractions and modified a few intemperate and inaccurate statements. I've also left in a very bits of commentary on the project's unfolding, as well as "100 Poem-Book"'s introduction, which was posted on Monday, January 28, 2008.

100 Poem-Books

So who's my intellectual hero, now that Guy Davenport's dead? Gotta be Jonathan Mayhew. I get a jittery shot of monkey glands every time I read his blog "Bemsha Swing," or at least get inspired to do something new. Right now Jonathan's kick-starting his novel-reading by blogging 100 novels—no particular list, no particular order, just whatever direction his nose takes him. So I'm going to play junior copy-cat, and see how long it takes me to blog 100 books of poetry. (Tag: 100 poem-books.) Like Jonathan, no rules, no lists, just whatever hits me; re-reads count, as do books I've been working at for months. It'll help clear out some of the vast "unread" shelves, at least.

1. Ed Roberson, *Atmosphere Conditions* (Sun & Moon, 2000)

I've got a small stack of Roberson I've been meaning to dive into, but this is the first of his "mature" volumes I've read. A strong, very moving book. The delicate, energetic tracing of thought—tentative and recursive—social and political anomie, sensual longing, the complexities of musical and cultural lineages: all played out in precise, thoughtful, flexible forms. Begins with Olsonian meanderings, perhaps too tentative to "grab" overtly, but grows more and more powerful as it proceeds, until you close the thing wanting immediately to start all over again.

2. Laynie Browne, *Rebecca Letters* (Kelsey St. Press, 1997)

Three longish sequences, mostly—though not strictly—prose poetry. A comfortable word order and syntax; these are for the most part standard sentences, save for the sorts of fragments one familiarly encounters in semi-formal writing ("The story of the ghost. The story of Rebecca."). The title sequence, "Rebecca Letters," is the longest and most striking, hovering around the Rebecca Browne (the poet's great-grandmother?) whose 1898 photograph appears on the cover. A dream of an "other history," a dream of language in which undefined "he"s, "you"s, and "she"s move on the fringes of consciousness. The shock of strangeness in the individual lexical choices ("curling circlets of rain") and in the movement from sentence to sentence, sometimes accretive, logical, sometimes sharply disjunctive. "A Sliding ontology." A dream of recovering the past, recovering memory, "a web to be reunited": "Is there a dependable urn into which I might deposit the results of all that has been burned?" An insinuative art too subtle to be summarized.

3. Alan Halsey and Karen Mac Cormack, *Fit to Print* (Coach House / West House, 1998)

A transatlantic collaboration between English (Halsey) and Anglo-Canadian (Mac Cormack) poets, *Fit to Print* takes the newspaper—its squished columns, its typos, its sometimes hilarious juxtapositions—as formal inspiration. All great fun, particularly in tracking Halsey and Mac Cormack's thefts and plunderings from the daily repository of pathos and inanity, though the two-columned form in which the book is set (appropriately enough) sometimes makes my eyes wuzz. I give the edge to Halsey's contributions, if only because I find his whimsy a trifle more congenial than what sometimes seems too earnest in Mac Cormack's pages, but I respect her keen eye for the economic and political implications of the *Globe and Mail*'s quotidian cubist epic.

4. Rae Armantrout, *Next Life* (Wesleyan UP, 2007)

Poems so spare and taut one is afraid at first glance they'll evaporate from the page. But then, as one finds oneself caught in the double imperative to read onward, to find out what comes next, and at the same time to read more and more slowly, so achingly slowly that the lines might as it were slow down and run backward, the incredible strength and cunning of Armantrout's work becomes evident: the unfailing keen eye for the everyday detail, the steel architecture of dizzyingly precise syntax. The poems are all bones, sinews, and corded muscle, spare machines of observation and groping, musical thought.

5. Robert Duncan, *Roots and Branches* (1964; New Directions, 1967)

Looking back at my poems a couple years ago, I was astonished at how deeply my own modes and formal conceptions had been shaped by an early reading of Duncan's late work—from *Bending the Bow* forward, especially the sequence "Passages." Surprising then it's taken me so long to make my way—after many abortive starts, much reading here and there—completely through *Roots and Branches*. So much that puts me—reticent, Protestant, skeptical, puritanical (?)—off: the operatic emotionalism, the wide-eyed mysticism, the persistent play with theosophical themes. All of which, to other eyes, could be seen as among the very *glories* of Duncan's poetry. I'm still divided, but find it impossible to gainsay the vatic *power* of the verse, the continual sense of a keen mind striving at questions on the very verge of knowledge, the exquisite modulations of a Romantic lyric voice almost unsurpassed in the twentieth century.

6. Nathaniel Mackey, *Splay Anthem* (New Directions, 2006)

I've been following the nomadic wanderings of Nathaniel Mackey's sequences *"mu"* and *Song of the Andoumboulou* for a couple of decades now, through his first three volumes of poetry—*Eroding Witness*, *School of Udhra*, and *Whatsaid Serif*—watching as they've circled around one another, coiled, braided, and finally, in this magnificent latest volume, virtually merged. I'll admit I've put off reading *Splay Anthem* for some months, for wholly selfish reasons: Mackey's simply so good, the dense and tasty music of his verse so entrancing, his play with pun and anagram so fertile, that whenever I spend time with one of his books I find myself irresistibly drawn to slavish (and mawkishly inferior) imitation. Like *School of Udhra* and *Whatsaid Serif*, much of the early part of *Splay Anthem* follows its speaker(s) through a dreamlike, surreal, cross-cultural pilgrimage, always surprising, always lively. It's tactilely rich, smelly, and consistently disorienting—rather like being astonished by what Don Cherry and Ed Blackwell will come up with next on the Mu albums that are one of *"mu"*'s referents. The real surprise in *Splay Anthem*, however, is the horrid spiritual and geopolitical stasis of the final section, "Nub"—"the imperial, flailing republic of Nub the United States has become," Mackey writes— one of the most impressive and horrifying visions of George Bush's America one could imagine.

7. Susan Howe, *Souls of the Labadie Tract* (New Directions, 2007)

Vintage Howe, in many ways: to my ears, less impressive than *The Midnight* but more moving than *Pierce-Arrow*. The method is of a piece with her earlier works, the evocation or reanimation of angular or marginalized voices form the past, whether the eighteenth-century Utopian Quietist (note to New Directions jacket-copy-writer: not "Quietest") Labadists, or the insurance lawyer and executive (and sometime poet) Wallace Stevens. For Howe the truly obscured voices—though I haven't lived with this book long enough to assert this with any assurance—are female: Stevens's wife Elsie (model for the Liberty dime), the women Labadists, Jonathan Edwards's wife Sarah Pierpont, a fragment of whose wedding dress the exceedingly fragmentary textual scraps of the final poem—"Fragment of the Wedding Dress of Sarah Pierpont Edwards"—circle around.

The proportion of prose to verse is lower than in Howe's earlier books, the paratexts framing the poetry proper less extensive and developed. In earlier writings such as the long poems collected in

The Nonconformist's Memorial (my own favorite), the "explanatory" prose sections and the more oblique verse sections had been more closely interwoven, what might be regarded as the prosaic "frames" interrupting and even impinging upon the exceedingly dense "poetic" sections. In *Souls*, in contrast, the prose lays the scene for each poem—the Utopian community of the Labadie Tract, Wallace Stevens's home at 118 Westerly Terrace, Hartford—then retreat before the poems proper. It is as if Howe were drawing back from the generic cross-cutting of her earlier poems, reforming her poetics—like some twenty-first-century Puritan—into a purer, simpler, more nakedly scriptural generic mode.

8. John Godfrey, *Midnight on Your Left* (The Figures, 1988)

Zap! Pow! Biff! I need an occasional shaking, like this volume of John Godfrey's, to remind me that poetry isn't all the serious exploration of historical antinomian impulse, of subterranean currents of occluded counter-speech, of the ever-deferred wanderings of nomadic cultural impulse. Sometimes it's sloppy (but precise), urbane (and oh so urban, even gritty), super-sexy, funny, and just plain *fun*. Godfrey's got a great ear, evident especially in his short-lined lyrics, and he's got a keen (if sometimes scopophilic) eye and analytic mind. So who's to gainsay him if the poems of *Midnight on Your Left* spend more time in the region of the crotch than the rafters of philosophical analysis? At any rate, I'm chalking this one down for possible inclusion in the "postmodern eroticism" project that I might get around to one of these years. The flâneur as cruiser: the poetry of (carnal) knowledge.

9. August Kleinzahler, *The Strange Hours Travelers Keep* (Farrar, Straus and Giroux, 2003)

This one won the 2004 Griffin Prize, the big Canadian jackpot. And good for August K., I say. I've been reading him—never religiously, always with pleasure—for over twenty years now, since Guy Davenport told me (on a blurb to *Storm Over Hackensack*) that his poems were "structures as cunningly built as kites and canoes." I suppose some of my friends would toss Kleinzahler into whatever oubliette of their imagination corresponds to Ron Silliman's "school of quietude"—and it's true that K's working in a sturdy, straightforward idiom that's essentially similar to what William Carlos Williams forged eighty-five years ago. But his ear for music is so strong, his diction is so aggressively varied, and he never lingers too much on himself: the world outside—its sights, noises, smells, songs, minute particulars—is so interesting that the last thing Kleinzahler wants to do is lament his own fuckups or celebrate his own sensitivity. A lot of travel poems here, and some of them it's true come perilously close to the "I'm lonely on a reading tour" subgenre. But Kleinzahler's scorn for the prima donna aesthete stance is so acidly evident that even a poem about the yearly shutting-down of an artists' colony—"The Art Farm"—reads like a savage indictment, without a single explicit word. A nature poet, but his nature's urban.

10. Melanie Neilson, *Natural Facts* (Potes and Poets, 1996)

Way back in the day in Ithaca, Melanie Neilson was one of the poets of "my" generation that Ted Pearson kept telling me to read. So I read *Civil Noir* (Roof, 1991), and enjoyed it. Bits of *Natural Facts* (love the r&b resonance of that title, combined with the Ralph Waldo Emerson of *Nature*) are explicit sequel to *Civil Noir*; other bits make use of some of the same overtyping and manuscript presentation. A big sense of humor here, a willingness to indulge in some serious slapstick among all that disjunction. And not that kind of allusive, highbrow-political Benjamin-quoting that starts the chuckles among the brow-furrowing reading-audience crowd, either. Real guffaws. All senses in play here.

11. Patrick Pritchett, *Antiphonal* (Pressed Wafer chapbook, 2008)

An odd rush almost of nostalgia reading this nicely-produced, cleanly laid-out, and precisely but passionately written chapbook—a sense of the idioms and concerns of the *Apex of the M* crowd back in those "how the hell do we get out from under the shadow of the Language Poets?" days, that heady mixture of post-Black Mountain, post-Objectivist poetics, Jabès- and Derrida-inflected narratives of loss and deferral, and Levinasian (or Samperian) reachings toward the numinous, the spiritual. My inner Zizek (or Hume) snorts: my inner Robert Duncan, enthralled by the cumulative music especially of the latter poems of *Antiphonal*, is delighted, just delighted, and moved.

12. Devin Johnston, *Sources* (Turtle Point Press, 2008)

Hey, this one's a set of uncorrected proofs—how often do you see *that* in the poetry world these days?—so don't look for the full color version until Turtle Point releases the book in September or so. I'm keen to see what the omnipresent Jeff Clark has done with the cover, but the interior design and typesetting is exquisite as usual. Johnston is of course one of the movers behind the always excellent Flood Editions, and the poems of *Sources* are almost a continuation of the aesthetics of Flood books: clean, lithe, spare, and quirky. "After Propertius" is tremendous. "The Pipe" amused me at first as a reprise of Mallarmé's prose poem "La Pipe," in which the accidental discovery of a pipe throws the Frenchman's imagination back to his London days—then I realized, from its "charred bowl and thatched screen," that Johnston's is *that* kind of pipe, not the tobacco sort.

13. Novalis, *Hymns to the Night*, translated by Dick Higgins (3rd ed., MacPherson and Co., 1988)

Apart from Schlegel's fragments, a couple volumes of Hölderlin, and a few of Goethe's lyrics, German Romanticism is *terra incognita* to me. Who woulda thought that Dick Higgins, Fluxus artist and the guy behind Something Else Press, had translated Novalis's gloomy prose poetry and free-verse set of death-meditations? The translations strike me as solid enough, if not particularly felicitous sometimes; Higgins translates into a kind of colorless contemporary English, rather than the ersatz "Romantic" diction one encounters way too often in this field, but he's no Richard Sieburth or Christopher Middleton. And my cold fish inability to buy into the Romantic excess of it all leaves me a bit chilly—though I'm intrigued by some of Novalis's reworkings of mythological and Christian material

14. Samuel Menashe, *New and Selected Poems*, edited by Christopher Ricks (Library of America, 2005)

Samuel Menashe's preface to this volume in the Library of America's "Poets Project," winner of the Poetry Foundation's "Neglected Masters Award," underscores what I've suspected for a long while: that S. M.'s been getting a hell of a lot of mileage out of his own "neglected" status—this despite the fact that he's been well-published in England, and that Talisman House brought out a "new and selected" volume almost as compendious as this one no further back than 2000. Stop whining, I think: Blake had it a lot worse.

But Menashe's undeniably got an idiom all his own, a mode that I find more impressive in long stretches than in brief batches (*pace* Christopher Ricks's over-clever introduction, which wants to show us that every Menashe lyric holds "eternity in a grain of sand"). Menashe's little poems aren't quite epigrams, nor do they have the gloomy gravitas of William Bronk's little poems; they certainly aren't haiku-like, nor do they have the slipshod, tossed-off likableness of many of Cid Corman's poemlets. They're uniformly clever, and sometimes—rather often—quite moving. Still, for micro-machines made out of words, give me

> the
> desire
> of
> towing
>
> any day.

15. Sophocles, *Ajax*, translated by John Tipton (Flood Editions, 2008)

I haven't read my way through the corpus of Greek tragedy, and *Ajax* was new to me before picking up John Tipton's energetic, precise new version of the play. Tipton's lodestars here are Christopher Logue's wonderful, anachronism-laden versions of the *Iliad* (though Tipton has the advantage over Logue of actually knowing Greek), Louis and Celia Zukofsky's "homophonic" translation of Catullus, and (though Tipton oddly doesn't mention it in his afterword) Zukofsky's five-word-per-line version of Plautus' *Rudens* ("A"-21). Tipton renders the Greek hexameters into six-word lines (except of course for the choruses, whose various meters he shifts into other word-counts): there's not the slightest hint of translatorese here, just a muscular, sensitive contemporary American English that packs an emotional impact I've only rarely encountered in translations of classical drama (one gets flashes of it in Pound's Sophocles versions). The story itself—which opens with Ajax, possessed of a divine madness, having slaughtered a herd of domestic animals, proceeds to his offing himself midway through the play, then ends with a debate over his burial—is weird enough to be compelling in the most prosaic rendering. Tipton's late-modernist idiom makes it oddly magnificent.

16. *Beowulf*, translated by Seamus Heaney (Farrar, Straus, and Giroux, 2000)

I think I read chunks of *Beowulf* in high school; I'm sure I read at least a graphic novel adaptation of it (or "comic book," as we used to say), as well as John Gardner's novel *Grendel*, narrated from the monster's point of view (though I remember nothing of that one but the cover art). I recall learning about kennings and ring-givers, but—laboring under the disadvantage of being an American—I never had a go at the Old English itself, even in college, where I read the thing through at some point (*not* for a course) in Burton Raffel's translation.

Seamus Heaney's version of the poem won prizes and praises, and I gather is now the text for the Norton Critical Edition. I'm sure he needs the money. Its sounds pretty Heaneyesque to me throughout, which moves me neither one way nor the other. I'd forgotten what a wonderful subject-jumper the Beowulf-poet is, how much trouble he has keeping his attention on the matter at hand. Guy Davenport did Old English with Tolkien at Oxford, which he would later recall in nightmares. Haven't seen the movie yet.

17. *Pure Pagan: Seven Centuries of Greek Poems and Fragments*, translated by Burton Raffel (Modern Library, 2004)

I seem to be on a classics/translations track lately. Nothing offensive, but very little memorable either about these version of classical Greek lyric. Indeed, there seems to be a strong scent of "sweepings," which is perhaps explained by Raffel's professed desire to avoid redoing poems more strikingly translated by Dudley Fitts, Guy Davenport, Mary Barnard—in other words, to try to find some decent leavings in an already pretty well-gleaned field. Drinking, death, bravery—not nearly enough sex. Guy D. contributes a scattered introduction, a fair specimen of his late, unfortunate essay style—all over the place but very occasionally to the point. Heart not in it.

18. Christopher Middleton, *Tankard Cat* (Sheep Meadow, 2004)

Anthony Cronin subtitles his Beckett biography "the last modernist" (a phrase I savagely wanted for my Louis Zukofsky biography), but of course neither L. Z. nor S. B. is the "last" in the modernist tradition. Me, I have a deep fondness for poets still working in the knotty, polyreferential, full-blown hi-octane modernist tradition. Not all of them are named "John," but John Matthias and John Peck are two of the best. And Christopher Middleton, who must have recently turned eighty, just keeps getting better and better. The poems of *Tankard Cat* range from simple and pellucid to mid-strength dense, but they're all shot through with the same musicality and sharpness of eye, nose, and palate, and informed by the same keen intelligence. Cosmopolitan—"world citizen"—poetry at its best.

19. Elizabeth Robinson, *Apostrophe* (Apogee, 2006)

Robinson is prolific—I know I've read several of her books and chapbooks, there are at least a half-dozen I've never laid eyes on. I suppose for me one of the most compelling elements in the two or three generations of poets that have come in the wake of Language Poetry has been the attempt to reinvent the *religious* poem, the poem addressing the numinous. (Cf. the "Apex of the M" phenomenon, and maybe that's one of the big things at stake somehow in the celebrated Watten/Duncan dustup of 1978.) Robinson does it as compellingly as anyone I know. The poems of *Apostrophe* seem to breathe a kind of oblique faith, an openness to the divine, less Christian or even Buddhist than simply, delicately *gnostic*. Few big gestures here—an unruffled surface of language chosen with almost obsessive care—but very lovely nonetheless.

20. Tom Pickard, *Ballad of Jamie Allan* (Flood Editions, 2007)

I've always cherished and respected Tom Pickard as the young chap who jump-started the elderly Basil Bunting's career, but I've always felt that there was an element of special pleading in the Baz's extravagant praise of Pickard's early work. Some of it, it's true, was a wonderful kind of drug-era updating of the Northern ballad tradition; a lot of it just didn't move me. The recent run of Flood Editions Pickard titles—a new and selected poems, *The Dark Months of May*, and now *Ballad of Jamie Allan*—have changed my mind: count me in with Bunting's shade as a full-fledged Pickard booster. *Jamie Allan* is really quite wonderful: the reconstruction of the life of an eighteenth-century Northumbrian piper, horse-thief, and general ne'er-do-well, told through a collage of legal documents, newspaper reports, impressionistic first-person lyrics, and wonderful ballads. It's a mixture that constantly seems on the verge of falling apart into scrapbookery, but which miraculously hangs together, and rings in the mind afterward.

21. cris cheek, *The Church—The School—The Beer* (Plantarchy, 2007)

The method by which these transcribed talk pieces were produced is almost too complex to go into. cris cheek spent an hour a day walking around downtown Norwich in a nice gray suit, talking into a hand-held CB radio transmitter while listening to various texts piped into his earphones; simultaneously, he was being filmed from across the street, where auditors could listen to his live transmissions and watch a video feed. (There's much more, which I won't even try to describe.) At any rate, the published transcriptions—no doubt a pale shadow of the several-ring media circus this project was—a wonderful mingling of overheard conversation, sociological speculations, immediate observations, and sheer *rambling*, are a wonderful read. No one composes on his feet like cris cheek does. Is it "poetry"? Who the hell cares.

22. William Fuller, *Watchword* (Flood Editions, 2006)

Damn, William Fuller is one *weird*, fascinating poet. My own tendency is toward the musical, the lyrical, whether in the complex, baroque musics of Bunting, the bare dissonances of Zukofsky, or the super-lush organ-tones of Ronald Johnson, Swinburne, or Milton. Fuller's poems are so dissonant that I want to call them not just alyrical, but anti-lyrical. Nonetheless, for all their syntactic dead ends, their strange and abrupt shifts of register, their abstractions resting cheek-by-jowl with their vivid images—or perhaps *because of* all those things—the poems of *Watchword* are as imperatively readable—that is, they force you to read, and read on, and read again—as anything I've opened in the last year. I find this stuff hard to describe: maybe imagine Thomas Traherne crossed with some seventeenth-century philosopher, crossed with a particularly eloquent writer of legal briefs—but with an extraordinarily loose sense of syntax, and a keen eye for the visible and invisible worlds.

23. Christopher Middleton, *The Tenor on Horseback* (Sheep Meadow, 2007)

Everything I said about Middleton the other day—particularly the part about his just getting better and better—still applies. *Tenor* is a somewhat less hefty collection than *Tankard Cat*—considerably shorter, many of the poems more ostensibly "slight"—a number of them almost "found" bits of dialogue, short observations, or anecdotes. But the poem-by-poem density of language and sharpness of thought is very high indeed. The title piece is of all things a theodicy, a meditation on the problem of existence and of human suffering; it's an amazing performance, a perfect thing of its kind.

24. Lisa Jarnot, *Night Scenes* (Flood Editions, 2008)

Ever notice how rare it is these dark days to come upon a book of really *happy* poems? I get the sense from *Night Scenes* that Lisa Jarnot is at a really good place in her life, and the poems that have resulted—some of them rhymed, some sonnets, a few oulipian procedural things, an "imitation" or two—make me really happy, make me smile. Her afterword—nodding to three of the best of her contemporaries, Elizabeth Willis, Lee Ann Brown, and Jennifer Moxley—makes it clear that *Night Scenes* is out to recapture some of that early joy and excitement in poetry that I for one sometimes feel I've lost. And it's a success.

25. Anthony Barnett, *Poem About Music* (Burning Deck, 1974)

Although I have a handful of his books, I know little about Anthony Barnett. He seems to have been instrumental in promoting—or introducing—Zukofsky's work to the French poets back in the day (the first page of *Poem About Music*, I'm convinced, is a nod to L. Z.); he published Prynne, and the collected poems of Veronica Forrest-Thomson; he's a jazz violin aficionado, and runs a jazz fiddle (and poetry) website which is one of the very few sites to which Paul Zukofsky's record label's site links. *Poem About Music* is a long poem with very few words, sometimes only one word to a page; and many of those words aren't Barnett's but Charles Olson's or Charles Montagu Doughty's. The Doughty, at least, gives long stretches of the poem—if one can speak of "long stretches" in a work this delicate and evanescent—a somewhat archaic, "literary" flavor. The whole thing reminds me strongly of early John Taggart or mid-period Theodore Enslin: the pursuit, at all cost, of the poem as *literal* music.

26. Stephen Vincent, *Walking Theory* (Junction Press, 2007)

When I was in Ithaca, and later when I was in suburban Virginia, I used to take seemingly endless, aimless walks—a clearing or focusing of the mind, a leaving-behind of the problems on my desk to immerse myself in the atmosphere of outside, and in a steady physical rhythm. The South Florida heat, a full-time job, and two small children have largely put an end to that habit, but Stephen Vincent's *Walking Theory* makes me hanker to strap on the New Balances and head out in no particular direction.

The "walk poem" is something of a subgenre all its own, as my old Cornell pal Roger Gilbert explored in his highly readable critical study *Walks in the World*. For a lot of people, A. R. Ammons's "Corson's Inlet" is the epitome of the species, but I've always thought of Zukofsky's "A"-13, with its stroll along the Brooklyn Promenade, conversation between L. Z. and his son interspersed with all manner of current events, concrete observations, and the general kitchen-sink bolus of cultural materials that Zukofsky brings to bear on the quotidian.

Stephen Vincent's walk-poems lean more toward the Zukofskyan than the Ammonsesque end of the spectrum, but they're more rooted in his surroundings, more alive to the immediate impressions around him than the myopic, astygmatic L. Z. ever was: "site/sight" is a repeated mantra here. Astonishingly how capacious the walk becomes in Vincent's poetics, becoming the vehicle for celebration, for painful elegy, for painful rumination. Impressively *human* poetry. Somebody I'd enjoy taking a walk with.

27. Elizabeth Arnold, *Civilization* (Flood Editions, 2006)

The classics are everywhere these days. (In my parents' house, I took down from Dad's shelves C. M. Bowra's *The Greek Experience*, conscious again of what a foreign country Greek and Latin culture is to me.) Elizabeth Arnold flirts with the classics—a bit of Archilochos and Apollonius, various archaeological digs and Mediterranean landscapes—and juxtaposes those fragments of a lost world with the crumbling edifice of individual human memory: of a father in a nursing home, sliding down the long, painfully gradual incline into complete amnesia. Civilization itself is really no more than group memory, jealously guarded, fought for and passed down. Memory, individual and collective, is what makes us human. Perhaps it's just me—the sadness of these precise, careful poems is almost too much to bear.

28. William Bronk, *Manifest; And Furthermore* (North Point, 1987)

This may be my favorite of the Bronk books I've read so far. Okay, sure, it's still obsessed with the "big" questions of the meaning of life (meaningless), the reality of the world (indeterminable), the place of humanity (an infinitesimal specklet); and he's still given to positing it all in terms of a "we" that I instinctively draw back from (*we who?*, Mr Bronk, I keep saying). But there's a coy humor and a variety of voice in the poems of *Manifest* that seem to fade from W. B.'s later volumes, and even—*mirabile dictu*—the intimation of other human beings, as if the whole exercise might be part of a dialogue or conversation, rather than heroic and despairing Bronkisms uttered in the face of the unechoing void. In "Manner of Speaking"—

> So much of what we say is, as we say,
> a way to say it. Those not content with that
> may begin to believe what is said. Even, at times,
> the speakers do. Better is what they should know.

—one even gets a taste of the pithy wisdoms of that diminutive Zen master Yoda.

[Blogging my way through 100 poem-books is really a pretty damned arbitrary exercise, no? But it's turning out to be rather more fun that I thought it would be. Trying to avoid obiter dicta and blurbisms (with varying success): perhaps merely reading notes to myself, in the end.]

29. John Tipton, *Four Fables* (Answer Tag Home Press, 2007)

Four poems on ancient themes in this very brief, very beautifully-produced chapbook. "Medea" and "Ajax," sonnets in seven-word lines that update their subjects Christopher Logueishly, bookend. In between are "The Mark," spoken in the voice of Cain, and "Chased," a gripping bit of Herodotus. Tipton's prosody gets sparer and sparer, and his voice more and more resonant.

30. Joel Felix, *Monaural* (Answer Tag Home Press, 2007)

This chapbook of poem and drawings (very fine ones, by Wallace Whitney), out of the Chicago-based Answer Tag Home Press, is in what I believe is known as an "accordion" binding, where a couple of sheets of paper are folded again and again to make successive pages. It's a thing of beauty to hold, and look at. And, one might add, to read and re-read. *Monaural* is, as Joel Felix explains, "a single output from multiple inputs," and I'm impressed and amused by the sensibility that will splice together ancient Roman epitaphs, the results of a children's questionnaire on the afterlife, and the Blues Brothers (of all things). Expansive but lapidary.

31. William Wordsworth and Samuel Taylor Coleridge, *Lyrical Ballads* (New Riverside Editions, 2002)

I've almost certainly read all the poems in the 1798 *Lyrical Ballads*, some of them many times indeed, but this is the first time I've read them straight through in the order of their first, anonymous collection, as presented in this handy New Riverside Edition edited by William Richey and Daniel Robinson (it also includes about 300 pages of background materials and contemporary critical reactions). I think I'll be using this book for an "Introduction to Literary Studies" course this fall, so expect ongoing comments on the editing, its strengths and shortcomings. For the nonce, however, I get a "Tintern Abbey"-like sensation of pleasurable homecoming at returning to these poems. Consider me a wholly uncloseted Wordsworth fan, as much for the (mawkish?) ballads as for the personal, pseudo-philosophical blank verse things.

32. Daniel Bouchard, *Sound Swarms and Other Poems* (Slack Buddha Press/La Perruque Editions, 2004)

What sticks in my mind from the poems in this chapbook of Daniel Bouchard's is a kind of wonderful serene thoughtfulness that places in lyric suspension the minute particulars of nature—some very keenly observed birds here, and a good deal of weather—and the human environment of roads, houses, and familial relationships. The last three poems—"Some Mountains Removed," "Sound Swarms," and "The Fancy Memory" (walk-ons by William Blake—"get your damn feet off the sofa"—F. D. R., and Abraham Lincoln) propose, in a quietly surrealist idiom, an entire theory of the relations between vision (poetic, political) and power. "I asked Lincoln how he felt about being called 'Captain.'"

33. Geraldine Monk, *She Kept Birds* (Slack Buddha Press/La Purruque Editions, 2004)

A dandy little chapbook from one of the most reconditely interesting contemporary English poets, *She Kept Birds* is something of an avian *80 Flowers*. Each of these twenty-one short-lined (often one word per line) poems is titled with the Linnaean binomial for a particular bird, and the text that follows is culled in various ways—I take it—from a birding handbook. It's wonderful how Monk plays registers and derivations off one another, giving the reader—in a remarkably *spare* text—a sense of the history and vernacular *weight* that these birds carry in the British Isles. English as birdsong.

34. Richard Howard, *Without Saying* (Turtle Island, 2008)

Richard Howard writes dramatic monologues, sturdy and subtle, historical or literary characters telling little stories. It's not work I seek out, or linger over; I always read his poems with pleasure, but am rarely moved. Sometimes I find myself comparing them, to their detriment, with Guy Davenport's stories: I'll take Guy's "Aeroplanes at Brescia" (Kafka almost meets Wittgenstein) over Howard's "Only Different" (Henry James almost meets L. Frank Baum) any day. The best piece is "Pederasty," a leering little sonnet after Proust.

35. K. Lorraine Graham, *Terminal Humming* (Slack Buddha Press/La Perruque Editions, 2004)

The title of Graham's chapbook, judging from the cover art—the instantly recognizable "male/female" bathroom icons, flanking the highway icon indicating an airport—would seem to refer to the exhilarating babel of conversations, languages, and linguistic registers in which one is immersed at the airport. And Graham's poems, which consistently surprise and delight, beautifully capture the effect of the constantly shifting, densely cross-grained linguistic environment of any public place in the early twenty-first century. But the title bears darker implications: that the "humming" of voices which surround us is an index of Late Capital's "terminal" status, that the "white noise" of our environment—as in DeLillo—is no more or less than a numbingly complex death rattle. The opener,

"Love Poem," encapsulates the American consumerist libido:

> And I want
> And I want
> And I want *baaaaah*

36. Graham Foust, *As in Every Deafness* (Flood Editions, 2003)

The short-lined free verse lyric, as worked out in the twentieth century by such folks as Zukofsky, Williams, Robert Creeley, A. R. Ammons, Cid Corman, Frank Samperi, etc., runs its own set of risks and offers its own rewards. Both risks and rewards are on display in Graham Foust's first full-length collection.

By "short-lined *lyric*," of course, I mean something distinct from a merely short line, which can serve as the formal basis for much longer works (L. Z.'s "A"-19, for instance, or Samperi's or Ammons's various long poems): I mean a brief poem, rarely two full pages, in which the lines tend to hover around a four-word average, in which the proportion of blank space to printed paper is at times overwhelming. Mallarmé's *Un coup de dés* was the first great verbal exploration of the aesthetics of the isolated mark against the void of the blank page, but the weight of silence or nullity has long been an obsession of contemporary arts—think Arvo Pärt, Morton Feldman, John Cage, Brian Eno's *Music for Airports*, and any number of twentieth-century visual artists.

The most obvious effect of writing poems that are shards of language marooned in a sea of white paper—or scattered stars shining out of an otherwise empty sky, choose your metaphor—is that an almost unbearable weight is placed upon what few words do appear. At least this is the case in Foust's poems, which almost never have the insouciant, tossed-off quality of so many of Creeley's short lyrics. They're *composed*, sometimes almost painfully so.

More often than not, the poems work. Foust has a very good ear, and as importantly a strong—though not unerring—sense for the off-balance, the off-kilter and incomplete that saves them from becoming Bronkian reports on reality or Cormanesque cuff-jottings. I sense that Celan is a tempting model for Foust, as well—Celan, the singular master who's led so many young American poets into dead-ends of laconic portentousness—but Foust has a wonderfully light touch that enable him to nod to the German poet without falling into his gravitational black hole. *As in Every Deafness*—dark poems, but with a wry, slanted darkness that makes the reader smile uneasily, lines stuck in her or his head.

37. Graham Foust, *Necessary Stranger* (Flood Editions, 2007)

My last Foust post got pilloried [in the comments box] in ways that I didn't really have the energy to respond to, except to say that all I meant to imply by name-dropping all those "short-line short-poem" poets along with Foust was that (as I said) the form bears specific dangers and possible rewards, which can fall under various epithets: the "gnomic," the "epitaphic," "brevity as the soul of wit"—or the "portentous," the "squib"—and so forth. When you put a small *thing*—a set of words, a splotch of color, a cluster of tones—in the midst of a big stretch of *nothing*—white paper, blank canvas, silence—you automatically place a heavy weight of readerly / viewerly / auditorial attention on that *something*. The poetics of the haiku, or of nouvelle cuisine.

Problem I've always had with writing about poetry is that I tend to want to describe what's new to me in terms of what's familiar. And since I was trained as a formalist, I tend to think in terms of the gross physical forms of poems. Don't mean to imply that Foust's short-lined, short lyrics are equal to (or better than, or not as good as) Creeley's or Ammons's or whoever's—that needs to be settled on a poem-by-poem, collection-by-collection basis—if indeed one wants to spend the energy "settling" it. But the problem (or tactic) of semantic isolation and the concomitant semantic weight placed on the poem is common to everyone I named, however awkwardly or gracefully they negotiate it.

I like the poems of *Necessary Stranger*, Foust's third collection, a trifle better than *As in Every Deafness*. If anything, they're a bit more mannered than the earlier book—still given to terms of really unexpected weirdness, but with a few elements I didn't detect in the first outing. For one thing, there's a lot more open intertextuality of the "high culture" sort, hat-tipping to other, earlier poems (mostly, unsurprisingly, in a subversive manner). And then there's a new sort of minimalist groove going on—minimalist in the repetitive, Steve Reichian sense—the repetition of phrases and words within individual poems. All this, plus a kind of general broadening of Foust's scope and language in general, shows that he's not a poet who's standing still.

38. Lyn Hejinian, *Slowly* (Tuumba Press, 2002)

I'm always trying to catch up on my Hejinian-reading. *Slowly* is a short long poem, published by Hejinian's own Tuumba Press (resurrected?—dunno, but I miss those wonderful letterpress chapbooks from the old days). As the title would indicate, it's a poem about—or revolving around, or formally built upon—the *adverb*. I can't help thinking of all those workshop strictures on adverbs—I've thrown them around myself: you know, "if you're using an adverb that means you haven't found the right verb," "avoid adverbs, they drain energy from your language," etc. So there's some foundational cheekiness here I quite like. Of course, what Hejinian's really interested in, and what gets tracked through all those adverbs (yes, "slowly" appears quite often) is the process of perception, how the world comes to us modified by our senses, by the various grids and seines of our consciousness that can be represented on one level by the shorthand of the adverb.

Much of the book's in a series of the sort of paratactic, present-tense declarative sentences that I associate with some of Barrett Watten's and Ron Silliman's work. So much so that it's a kind of major event when Hejinian shifts into the past tense for a run of lines. A brow-furrowing read.

39. Peter Gizzi, *Some Values of Landscape and Weather* (Wesleyan University Press, 2003)

A splendid extravagance of language, a brilliant eye for colors and for details, the objects/detritus/treasured things of the visible. Yes, the reinvention of the "lyric," whatever that means (to cite one of Gizzi's blurbists)—or a loving caress of the body of the sensual world. A splendid extravagance of forms, as well, from reinventions of the *cante jondo* to love songs built on syntactic games. A far better elegy for Gregory Corso than one would expect—or than he perhaps deserves.

40. Peter Gizzi, *The Outernationale* (Wesleyan University Press, 2007)

Still rife with image and sound, but sparer, more tentative than Gizzi's previous volume. Notes of love, of celebration, yes, but more notes of disquiet, even despair. The syntax halts, takes a step beyond previous simplicity, not into a heightened Prynneian complexity or a Zukofskyan indeterminacy, but into incompletion, or truism. The Watts Towers, triumphant emblems of the homegrown bricoleur—focussed in their glory on the cover of the Living Batch press edition of Ronald Johnson's *ARK*—appear on Gizzi's cover at a precarious angle, brought down to earth in their scrubby context: a pickup truck, a panel van, an electrical pole, prefab buildings.

41. Joanne Kyger, *Not Veracruz* (Libellum, 2007)

Three months' worth (January–March 2006) of journal poems in this slim, generously designed book. I like Kyger's laid-back, sometimes cynical California-Buddhist sensibility, her ability to pull a joyful haiku-ish exclamation out of the clearing up of a clogged septic tank. Overheard language ("the world's sole remaindered superpower"), the static surrounding everyday life, all of it shadowed and bordered by the "war on terror" and other, more concrete wars.

42. John Matthias, *Kedging: New Poems* (Salt, 2007)

Matthias is one of the last true-blue high modernists, along with a handful of others, including Christopher Middleton and John Peck. And he's the most quotational, referential, and paratactic of the lot—in short, the most Poundian (or David Jonesian). Happily, he long ago cured himself of the Poundian-Olsonian urge to Make the World a Better Place Through Poetry, and can turn the machinery of association to the ends of instruction (we learn lots of stuff in these poems, about lots of sometimes arcane matters) and delight—and they're lots of fun, the big "Laundry Lists and Manifestoes" and "Kedging in Time," poems that form the core of this new collection. High spirits abound, but shot through with moments of piercing melancholia.

43. Lyn Hejinian, *The Beginner* (Tuumba Press, 2002)

Like the roughly contemporaneous *Slowly, The Beginner* is a short book from Hejinian's own Tuumba Press. I like this one very much indeed. An extended meditation on how we start things out: how a piece of writing gets begun and evolves into itself, how children "begin" to be human beings through various acts of "play," how we figure out where and what we are in the world. Passages of deep beauty.

There's no escape from these repeating units of incipience, these figs and catapulting confidences divulged by a world, one whose beginnings are arrayed all around and side by side.
I stand by the window, look out, and my "self" occurs, a manifestation of the world as that for which I yearn.
To be a self is simply to be something in the world and yet yearning for it.

Does this remind any else—as it does me, oddly, weirdly—of Ronald Johnson?

[Been having my doubts lately about this "100 poem-books" thing. Not sure, that is, what the use-value of the project is. Notes, obviously, too short to serve as serious "reviews," always in danger of falling into mere blurb-copy, the sort of stuff the *TLS* editors have an ongoing column feature devoted to making fun of. The fact is, I reflect drearily, that I'm too scattered to have much of substance to say about what I'm reading. Perhaps, as a bear whose very little brain is ill-fitted for pomo multi-tasking, I should spend less time watching poll sites, listening to five tracks apiece from four different albums, reading blogs, dipping into seven different books of literary criticism, scanning a chapter of Ruskin, playing the same song five times in a row on two different guitars, checking my e-mail—you get the picture—and buckle down to the serious business of mastering contemporary poetry. (We don't have cable, by the way, because we recognize it would mean the absolute end of my intellectual life, already under siege from a stack of DVDs.) What's the good of putting up a public snapshot of my futile efforts to get with it? I.e., to work my way through what was the hottest book among the cognoscenti—four years ago?]

44. Rodrigo Toscano, *Platform* (Atelos, 2003)

A biggish book of very exciting poems. Toscano reinvents, revitalizes the hortatory political poem in post-Language Poetry idiom. That is, these rousing and very funny poems are every bit as committed to a hard-Left politics as any of the soapbox-stompers from the 1930s that Cary Nelson's written about, but Toscano's a political poet who's read and absorbed his Brecht, his Gramsci, his Frankfurt School, his Hardt and Negri. Terry Eagleton's been arguing for a decade now that "postmodernism"—and what he means by the term is so broad it's almost risible, a branch to beat whatever thinker he's dissatisfied with at the moment—is *politically* a failure, that the multiple ironies and cynicisms of post-seventies critical discourse render their users unable to gain the firm purchase of the "real" that's necessary for meaningful political interventions. (Similar attacks have been leveled at the Language Poets themselves.) Toscano shows that it's possible to forge a new, every exciting, and very *alive* political poetry precisely out of the ironies and cynicisms that have become the lingua franca of the dissolving present.

Of course, it doesn't hurt that the man's a brilliant satirist, in the best Jonathan Swift-Monty Python-*South Park* tradition. Nobody—ardent humorless working Leftists, quietist poets, armchair academic Marxists, the whole post-avant literary establishment, and of course the phalanx of ghoulist plutocrats who run our government and economy—comes out of *Platform* unscathed. But it's not a self-dissolving, foundationless satire, either, but one that forces a reader to think through her/his own position, leaves a reader uncomfortable in the best Brechtian manner.

45. Alan Halsey, *Not Everything Remotely: Selected Poems 1978–2005* (Salt, 2006)

One I confess I've been lingering over for a long time, reading slowly and recursively, dipping in and about, alternately fascinated, baffled, seized with hilarity, always delighted. Stevens: "poetry is the scholar's art"; Coleridge's figure of himself (taken up by Susan Howe) as a "library-cormorant." Halsey, "specialist bookseller," deep scholar of the Romantics, editor of Thomas Lovell Beddoes, revises the terms:

poetry is the bookman's art. *Not Everything Remotely* is a core sample (*coeur simple?*) of twenty-seven years' worth of little and big collections from one of the five or six poets whose work I'll buy immediately on sight, no questions asked, without bothering to open the book or read the blurbs. Halsey's poems—and they come in such variety, from very straightforward, personal-voice addresses to the most recondite word salads—are like a dense portable anthology from a rich and complex literary canon that simultaneous overlaps with but is fundamentally shifted or twisted from the recognizable "canon"—from Linear B to J. H. Prynne. A marvelous "fake book"—fake errata sheets, fake pre-Sokratic fragments, fake emblems, fake dictionary entries—all at once wryly high-spirited, revelling in in-jokes and outrageous japes, and serious as a heart attack (a hart, a tack). The bones of English culture sea-changed into "something [Bridget Jones writes] v. v. rich, v. v. strange." And of course the unavoidable, undeniable question: "Who doesn't sometimes / need an hour when there's no / evading Swinburne?"

46. John Ashbery with Joe Brainard, *The Vermont Notebook* (1975; in Ashbery, *Collected Poems 1956–1987*, Library of America, 2008)

One of the grand old hold-outs, the Library of America has finally shifted over to a matte finish for their dust jackets; now only the author's name ("Calligraphy by Gun Larson") and the tricolor band remain in the traditional high-gloss finish. End of an era; oh well, I thought that when they started using full-color author portraits, as well. Nice to have thirty-plus years of Ashbery in one brick volume, though something just feels *wrong* about his making it into the series before Dickinson, Moore, William Carlos Williams, Oppen—well, we won't go on with names, will we? Wouldn't mind a Joel Barlow volume, either.

I don't know the back story on *The Vermont Notebook*. It feels like a vacation fancy, a fun collaboration between the poet (Ashbery) and the illustrator (Joe Brainard), setting Brainard's sketchy monochrome copies of photos in counterpoint to all manner of Ashbery ramblings: lists of products, shops, proper names, elements of the townscape; Steinian exercises in repetitive prose; reproduced magazine copy; even a real live *poem* or two. Pleasantly diverting, all in all—though I'm sure I'm not the only one to bemoan the LOA's bible paper in this case: while the Brainard drawings are reproduced (well) in gray, they glare through the recto of every bloody page.

47. Jay Wright, *Music's Mask and Measure* (Flood Editions, 2007)

I remember listening to the Zero Mostelish Harold Bloom pontificate away on some DC-area talk radio show (Diane Rehm?) a million years ago—it must have been in support of *The Western Canon*, perhaps his last book to show any trace of critical intellect. Even then, of course, he was deep into his Stanislavskian imitation of Samuel Johnson and was heading full speed into his current mode of "quote-and-dote" (Terry Eagleton's term) "criticism." But as he launched into a bitter (and frankly tired) assault on the "schools of resentment," I had one of those stopped-clock-tells-the-right-time-at-least-twice-a-day moments: yes, I found myself agreeing, Jay Wright is an incredibly good poet, and there aren't nearly enough people saying so.

Music's Mask and Measure is perhaps the most spare book of Wright's I've read. A series of short—mostly five- and six-line pieces disposed over five "equations," largely bare of proper names or specifiable reference. It's clear these are poems about music, and poems about dance: the "mask" is both a carnivalesque concealment and a stately entertainment. The "equations," though the drawings that head each section gesture toward African petroglyphs, would seem to refer back to Pythagorean number/musical lore. But what's the use?—I can't honestly say precisely what these poems are "about" (other than their own stately, nimble music), or what they "say" (other than their own stately, nimble music). Their syntax is simple, straightforward, their vocabulary precise and only occasionally recondite; but their reference is so oblique, so attenuated, that this bear of very little brain finds himself much at sea. Which is ultimately quite alright: it's the careful, sturdy, and surprising music that carries these poems past the point of mystery into a place of restrained and refined *jouissance*, or the moment just before, prolonged through fifty-odd pages of measured lyricism.

48. Barbara Guest, *The Red Gaze* (Wesleyan University Press, 2005)

A truism—by now, a cliché even—to speak of Guest's poems as "painterly." But they are, after all—poems acting and reenacting the "gaze" of the title, the act of seeing (the viewer's art) and the act of placing colors upon a field (the painter's). Spare poems, like a painter's spare palette, a canvas marked with only a few gestures of color—red, as the title (again) indicates, is prominent, though never saturating. Perhaps the most purely *aesthetic* poems I've encountered in some time: that is, poems grounded in the satisfactions of the senses, shutting out the social, the political, the historical even—or setting them far to one side to pursue the immediate gratification of the eyes.

49. Craig Watson, *True News* (Instance Press, 2002)

Three serial pieces—"Spectacle Studies," "Where/As," and "Home Guard"—that circle around geopolitical themes—interpreted as broadly as possible—"the personal is the political," politics colonizes/conditions consciousness, etc. A deft touch throughout, smart and lively. The four sections of "Where/As" are place-specific (Venice, South Africa, China, Ecuador), and bend their essentially similar forms to accomodate a vivid impression of each locale. Most exciting are the quatrain poems of "Spectacle Studies," which touch on stereotypically "big," abstract—even philosophical—questions with a sure hand and a clear sense of when the abstract becomes particular and vice-versa. Nice work; not as lyrical as the three or four Watson books I've read before.

50. Lisa Jarnot, *Black Dog Songs* (Flood Editions, 2003)

Given the Steinian provenance of much of her language, and her penchant for rollicking dactylic meters, it's no surprise that the tone of much of Jarnot's *Black Dog Songs* is very precisely *whimsy*. But she wears her whimsy with a difference—it's underlaid with melancholy, with constant reminders of the carnivorous nature of the doggies she so dotes upon, of the dark depression or even madness that can manifest itself in sing-song melodies. The sequence "My Terrorist Notebook" makes a wonderful, light-touched attack on post-9/11 American policy, while the prose poems (and one sestina) of "They" proffer an anthropology of the loves and likings of some unspecified race—"they"—which turns out to look very much like us. I still cherish a great attraction to the overwritten opacities of Jarnot's first volume, *Some Other Kind of Mission*, but I like Jarnot's whimsy more than anything this side of Stein herself, or Edward Lear.

51. Carolyn Forché, *Gathering the Tribes* (Yale University Press, 1976)

I've read most of Forché, backward—first *The Angel of History* (1994) a year or two after it came out, then *The Country Between Us* (1981) maybe 3 years ago, and only now her first book, *Gathering the Tribes*. (Haven't seen the most recent—2003—*Blue Hour*.) I've found them of diminishing interest, I guess, though I can't really muster much enthusiasm even for *Angel*. *Gathering* is very assured, intelligent writing, however: very, very good, of its kind. Stanley Kunitz's foreword leers embarrassingly, even for 1976 ("the outstanding Sapphic poem of an era").

52. Ron Silliman, *The Age of Huts (compleat)* (University of California Press, 2007)

There's something about Silliman's work that has always been just *there* for me—an element of the landscape, a big looming presence of possibility. I like the "compleat" *Age of Huts* better than the old Roof edition—as Zukofsky says somewhere, "more of a good thing." Though I don't think Ron would appreciate the comparison, I'm put in mind of the "fractal" character of Brian Eno's ambient stuff—ie, the experience of hearing the 61-minute *Thursday Afternoon*, in details, isn't different from hearing a six-minute extract: it's just that the former is *longer*. (That *longer*, however, is a pretty crucial difference.) A poetry which not only (in Auden's phrase) "makes nothing happen," but in which *nothing happens*. Or rather, nothing big, dramatic happens, only a constant flow of small-scale events. "A poem without development, without events, without end" ("2197"). Every time I read Silliman I start covering notebook pages with diagrams and numbers for some large-scale recombinative project which I never end up writing.

53. William Fuller, *Sadly* (Flood Editions, 2003)

If anything, even more disorienting that *Watchword*, and at the same time a trifle more laconic. Still, tremendous stuff. Fuller indulges his lyrical gifts rather less in this one. The last poem, "I Now Think I Was Wrong," is Wallace Stevens without all illusions, stripped of all gaiety:

> Returning to the spring, we see green on the surface
> of the water. This is not the earth. Stand still, monkey,
> do not run. None of us was ever here before.

54. Elizabeth Arnold, *The Reef* (University of Chicago Press, 1999)

Where *Civilization* wrestles with a father's dementia, *The Reef* deals with the poet's own bouts with (I take it) Hodgkin's lymphoma. Harrowing reading, though beautiful as well. I admire the ambition that leads her to release, as a first book, a single long sequence of poems. Much of what makes *Civilization* so compelling—for me—is only in embryo here.

55. Isabelle Baladine Howald, *Secret of Breath*, translated from the French by Eléna Rivera (Burning Deck, 2008)

Vast stretches of white space, one voice in roman type, in dialogue or counterpoint to another in italic. War, displacement; the state of the refugee, which is the common state of twentieth-century Europe. War, snow, movement, and the inevitability of a death, which lends an existentialist cast to everything that goes down. Not Celan but Trakl; not so much Bonnefoy as St.-John Perse. (But contemporary French poetry is one of my vast ignorances.)

56. Joshua Clover, *The Totality for Kids* (University of California Press, 2006)

To be read with a French dictionary at one's side, along with the latest guide to cultural theory. Honeycombed with referentiality, like a postmodern *Rock-Drill*, though I'm always glad to stumble over Warren Zevon and Roxy Music (oddly enough, the latter not indexed). The disturbing thought that dissent itself, at least in its poetic embodiment, may have reached the stage where only the face is left floating above the acid pit of self-dissolving irony, like the factory worker in the James Kelman story. Very French indeed; I kept repressing the impulse to put on a beret, buy a pack of Gauloises, and find a café where I could order a carafe of wine as I read—or to climb

a barricade, turn over a Peugeot, throw a cobblestone at something—
if I could determine what my target might be.

57. Jennifer Moxley, *The Line* (Post-Apollo Press, 2007)

The "line" between sleep and waking, at least in part; between intellection and emotion? The line as something followed, something toed. "I Walk the Line." The language "of the heart," an attempt to use the old tropes of consciousness, of affect, *seriously* again, *without irony*. Twenty-first Century Romanticism? The prose poem, but not the New Sentence: the unit of composition is the poem itself (one or two pages), often telling a narrative or a fragment thereof. A kind of clear-eyed "shimmer" to these pieces, a muted awkward grace that has them gnawing into the corner of one's readerly eye as one picks up the next book.

58. John Taggart, *There Are Birds* (Flood Editions, 2008)

I sought out John Taggart on my own, pulled off I-81 on one of those drives between Blacksburg and Ithaca way back when, looked him up in the phone book at a filling station, and paid the proverbial ephebe's first visit. A mentor? Something like that, though as Ron Johnson said of Zukofsky, "I don't think he liked my poetry much." That was okay. Of all the Taggart books I've accumulated over the years, *Loop* (Sun and Moon, 1991) stands out, if only because it's biggest—slice that one anywhere and you'll hit a fantastic poem. But *There Are Birds* is frankly his greatest achievement yet, a set of five substantial poems and few outriding "cadenzas." There're elegies: one for Zukofsky, one for Creeley, one for Robert Quine—who would've thought that John, the bop-saturated jazz fan, would also admire the guy who comes close to topping my pantheon of guitar heroes? "Refrains for Robert Quine," a painfully touching elegy that never once directly alludes to the circumstances of Quine's death—in grief over the death of his beloved wife, he took an intentional overdose of heroin—brings me to tears.

The centerpiece is the long and *very* strange "Unveiling/Marianne Moore," a poem of place (south central rural Pennsylvania) that is simultaneously an erotic fantasy (delicate, disturbing) about two red-haired virgins, Moore and Emily Dickinson, an homage to the Bartrams and other "nature boys," a horticultural poem, and much more.

If John Adams and Philip Glass evolved their own minimalist techniques into a kind of late Romanticism, Taggart has taken the austere repetitiousness of *Peace on Earth* and "The Rothko Chapel Poem" and has stripped it down to an angular, Second Vienna School lyricism. If he used to be Robert Fripp, now he's Fred Frith.

59. David Shapiro, *To An Idea: A Book of Poems* (Overlook, 1983)

I picked this up because I figured that anyone Jonathan Mayhew admires so extravagantly must have something going for him. So what kind of poet would Mayhew admire?, I thought as I opened it up: intelligent, of course; with a deep sense of literary tradition, maybe a massive rooting in Mallarmé; unendingly fresh verbal gifts, surprising the reader in almost every line; and with a great sense of humor, because I don't see Jonathan stomaching large repeated doses of one of those long-range gloomy types. And guess what? That's exactly how Shapiro turns out to be. I've gotta spend more time with this second-generation New York School stuff—it puts a spark in my step that's been sadly missing lately.

60. Andrew Marvell, *The Complete Poems*, edited by Elizabeth Story Donno (Penguin Classics, 1985)

Don't quite know how to blog, in a series that's usually fleeting comments on newish contemporary things, a "classic." Marvell *pour les enfants*: the bridge (to my ears) between the Metaphysicals and Dryden's couplet wit; co-worker with Milton, and author of a tremendous introductory poem to *Paradise Lost*, in which Marvell lavishly praises Milton's blank verse, even if he can't let go of rhyme himself; ardent Republican; later ardent suck-up (at least in print) to Charles II; author of a couple of endless topical satires, mostly incomprehensible to contemporary readers (Calvin Trillin to readers in 2350 CE); one of the greatest political poets in English, not least because of his painful grasp of the ambiguities of power (the "Horatian Ode"). By far the greatest garden poet before Finlay.

A handy edition, this Penguin; quite as good, if not as complete, as the Oxford Authors; high points for no-nonsense, non-condescending annotations. And a dandy cover illustration of "King Charles II being presented with a Pineapple by Mr Rose the Royal Gardener" (Thomas Hewart). Remind me to tell you the one about Louis Zukofsky's father, Whittaker Chambers, and the pineapple.

61. Kit Robinson, *Ice Cubes* (Roof, 1987)

Continuing my trundle through the West Coast Language Poet's collective biography, *The Grand Piano* (just finished volume five), I took down a couple of Kit Robinson's books. Of all the Grand Pianists, he and Steve Benson are the ones with whose work I'm probably least familiar. *Ice Cubes* is in three sections: "Up Early," a run of twelve-line poems (composed in early morning? limbering-up exercises?—at any rate, spare, tense, and intelligent); "Oleo," a series of longer-lined, five-lined stanza'd pieces, rather denser and more witty—I'm way keen on "Nesting of Layer Protocols":

> Theory has it the word came first. But you always
> have to take somebody's word for it. That word,
> built up over time with letters from various
> alphabets, edges polished by the erosion of speech,
> is itself a result.

—and the fifty or so pages of "Ice Cubes," poems in four-line stanzas, one word per line. A neat trick, the form placing equal emphasis on each word, forcing Robinson to make lexical choice "count." For the most part (as in the earlier sections) straightforward syntax, casual tone, but a light effect very unlike the sometimes ponderous Orientalism of Zukofsky's one-word-per-line passages.

> these
> cubes
> designed
> to
>
> cool
> your
> drink
> dissolve
>
> faster
> than
> sound
> thinking

62. C. S. Giscombe, *Prairie Style* (Flood Editions, 2008)

Cecil Giscombe and I go way, way back—too far back, it seems these days—to when he was a whole lot younger than I am now. I knew his daughter when she was a prelingual toddler (there's a poem dedicated to her in my first collection, *Anarchy*); now she's graduated from college. His poetry just gets better and better, as he works steadily and slowly (*Prairie Style* is only his fourth collection), but more and more perfectly. The African diaspora across the Great Plains, with conceptual side trips to Canada and Jamaica. Foxes and trains, both of them quick, intelligent, and indigenous. A soft, persistent, imperative, ironical voice, telling a tale of the tribe; but more specifically telling—as has always been Giscombe's obsession—telling the phenomenology of particular *places*. Giscombe is to the Midwest what Stevens was to Key West, Bishop to an American's Brazil, Olson to Goucester. (Olson, frankly, is the only direct influence on Giscombe of those three hat-plucked names.) The only thing I miss here, in these beautifully sculpted, eye-brow-raised prose poems, is C. S. G.'s peerless sense of *the line*.

63. Peter Gizzi, *Periplum and other poems, 1987–1992* (Salt Publishing, 2004)

Much earlier work than what I've read of Gizzi before. Trying on various voices, various idioms, all with some success. I love the almost Ashberyan discursiveness of "Deux ex Machina" and "Hard as Ash," tho I'm perhaps drawn more immediately to the fragmentary notations of the chapbook-length *Music for Films*. (Brian Eno gives this one its title, an album I've played so many hundreds of times times on vinyl that I've never felt the need to buy the CD—every note is there in my memory.) Nods to Spicer (of course), to Duncan. Is Peter Gizzi the preëminent male love poet of his generation? A fair bet.

64. Gertrude Stein, *Tender Buttons* (1914—any number of editions, this time through in the Carl Van Vechten-edited *Selected Writings*, Vintage 1947)

Too long—a couple of years at least—since I've reread this one, long enough for me almost to forget what a fantastic *Wunderkammer* of delights and surprises and puns and rhythms and implacably sensible nonsense this little book is. There should be birthday celebrations all over the world for its centenary five years hence, for it's as fresh now as the day it was first printed. It makes most of last century's American poetry, from the early L. Z. and Oppen down through

Black Mountain, the Beats, and much of the post-avant scene, seem immediately dated. Not irrelevant, mind, and not less than valuable— but *dated*.

65. Joseph Donahue, *Before Creation* (Central Park Editions, 1989)

I try not to lend books myself; my own copy of Joseph Donahue's first book, I admit with only a little shame, actually belongs to my grad school friend Patty Chu, lent to me more years ago than I care to admit. She's not getting it back, I'm afraid. So I've known Joe's work a deal longer than I've known Joe himself. There're some great short poems in here (I'm partial to "Lou Reed" and "Adam, In Hell") but the standouts are the long, multi-part pieces like "Transfigurations" and "Crania Americana," in which you can see Donahue's characteristic limpid mysticism beginning to emerge from a more familiar, more ordinary "American Surrealism." "Purple Ritual" is a gripping collision of childhood memories of growing up in Texas, the poet's early observations of President Kennedy, and an imagining of Lee Harvey Oswald strangely conflated with the singer Orpheus: the JFK assassination, perhaps the nearest recent history gets to real live Greek tragedy, a persistent textual ghost haunting much of *Before Creation*.

66. Joseph Donahue, *World Well Broken* (Talisman House, 1995)

Back in the mid-90s, someone in middle Tennessee was regularly funneling review (?) copies of new Talisman House, Sun & Moon, and Coach House books into a stall in an antique mall in Nashville, where I would come by a couple times a year and buy them all. I remember checking out with Joe Donahue's *World Well Broken*, anent which a blue-haired woman working the cash register commented to a friend, "Looka that—'world way-ull broken'—well, it surely is, isn't it?"

World Well Broken, aside from the opening "Opiate Phobia," entirely leaves behind short lyrics in favor of more expansive things. "Spectral Evidence" is like a course in hauntology, the ghosts of Maya Deren and Harry Smith popping up at every turn. "Christ Enters Manhattan" is tremendous, the Second Coming imagined as a horror movie scripted by William Blake and directed by Luis Buñuel.

67. Anne Portugal, *Quisite Moment*, translated by Rosmarie Waldrop (Burning Deck, 2008)

A slim but delightful chapbook. A series of fourteen nine-line poems, each with a single three-line footnote. The trick here—as in the title, which wants to be or once was "Exquisite Moment"—is that the first letters or syllables of each line seem to be missing, leaving a fertile lacuna for the reader to speculate on what came before, to fill in the blanks. As in "sing in the bedroom" ("cursing in the bedroom"? "musing in the bedroom"? "you-know-what-ing in the bedroom"?):

> end came
> ipitously
> cuss
> digiously strong
> kini
> nty
> retched out on
> ouch
> ton bedsheet

"Bedroom" gestured erotica to me—maybe that's my bent*—but here it's infected, distempered by the loppage of words, "stretched" to "retched," "touch" (?) to "ouch." I can't imagine the procedures Rosmarie W. went through to find English "equivalents" for the original French.

*my favorite of the "footnotes":
the Swiss well
it's their Swiss bent
love Switzerland

68. Charles Alexander, *Near or Random Acts* (Singing Horse Press, 2004)

A shy, unassuming charm to this volume; the first half is seventy seven-line, five-word-per-line sections, the second half a further run of such poems, this time interspersed with Alexander's notebook entries and notes on the manuscript and compositional process. An "opening-up," as it were. The parallels of the first seventy poems—"near or random acts"—with Zukofsky's *80 Flowers* are obvious (Alexander himself makes the connection in an author's note at the end): the word-count constraints, the quotidian nature of much of the material, (sometimes) the allusions. But Alexander's aren't L. Z.'s hyper-dense nuggets of impacted history, philology, and allusion, whatever inspiration he may have taken from Zukofsky's last completed work. Instead, they're rather airy, highly musical units, suffused more often than not with a quizzical wonder at the spectacle of the poet's growing young daughters. A rather rare thing for me lately, and a very welcome one—a book of unabashed and enthusiastic love.

69. Peter Cole, *Things on Which I've Stumbled* (New Directions, 2008)

Cole is an acclaimed translator of Hebrew and Arabic poetry. I was nuts about his first two books, *Rift* and *Hymns and Qualms*. This new one strikes me as more straightforward, more first-person—but still terrifically impressive. Plainspoken wit, lots of gestures toward traditional form, a questioning but always humble mysticism, drawing as much on Muslim as Jewish sources. A number of savage, bitterly funny critiques of Zionism. The long, dazzling title poem is Cole's wanderings through the materials stowed in the *geniza*—"a storeroom that holds worn out and discarded Hebrew texts"—of a Cairo synagogue, now held in Cambridge. A brilliant and haunting collage of bits and pieces, ritual texts, love poems, letters, everything. "Strange how I've become a modern / poet of a medieval kind—/ making poems for a different diversion, / as they point toward what's divine."

70. Kit Robinson, *The Champagne of Concrete* (Potes and Poets, 1991)

More expansive and formally various than *Ice Cubes*, the last Robinson book I read, yet also more funny, more testy, more politically acute. A wonderfully quirky, slanted set of observations of American corporate life. If Dilbert were taller, handsomer, had a penchant for memorable verbal formulations and social critique—and if he weren't a comic-strip character—he might be something like the Kit Robinson of this volume. "The world is the case / It's a brief case." The book's almost too smart for me to diminish it with a "great fun."

71. Janet Holmes, *Humanophone* (University of Notre Dame Press, 2001)

Various poems in various forms here: a number of quite personal lyrics (some very moving); some confrontations with literary texts (Dante, Keats); meditations on place. The centerpieces are three sequences on musical material: "Celebration on the Planet Mars," which explores the life and work of jazzman Raymond Scott; "Humanophone," on Charles Ives's father George, a Civil War bandleader and as much a visionary as his more famous son; and "Partch Stations," on the incomparable composer and instrument-maker Harry Partch—all three men who heard music that no one before had ever imagined, and sought new instruments to make it real.

I'm reminded in these three sequences of one of the modes of John Matthias (and Matthias's student Bob Archambeau): a poetic hearkening back to certain strains of the high modernist, in which the poet's goal is to hold up and display the shiny, odd byways of cultural history. Poems like these, at their best, stand alone—but they always seize the reader by the shirt: *here's something you might not know, might never have heard of, but it could change your life, were you to follow this trace—read these books, listen these recordings, look at these pictures!* Something fundamentally *generous* there.

72. Cole Swensen, *Ours* (University of California Press, 2008)

I was drawn to this one by its very subject matter—seventeenth-century French formal gardening, particularly the work of the landscape architect André Le Nôtre (from whose name Swensen gets her punning title). I know relatively little about the French formal tradition of landscapes, exemplified by Le Nôtre's work at Versailles and Vaux-le-Vicomte; I've been more interested in the transition between formal and "picturesque" styles that takes place in England over the eighteenth century, and gets thematized in Pope and others.

But I'm a sucker for gardening poems, and Swensen's evocations of Le Nôtre are rich with history, pondering deeply the implications of shaping the landscape, its plants and watercourses, along strictly geometric lines. What I increasingly found fascinating in Swensen's poem-sequence, however, was her sense of the sentence. Her sentences, that is, unfold with deceptively straightforward syntax, often enriched by internal rhymes and sound repetition. But as they unwind over multiple lines, they shift direction, rhetoric, and blossom out into something quite different from what they began as—often, something larger, more "metaphysical."

Much of the time, I think it's fair to say, Swensen's addressing a strict and neoclassical art (the formal garden, which owes more to Euclid than it does to Longinus, more to geometry than to the sublime) in an interestingly post-Romantic register. Where Marvell's Mower laments the sterility of those evenly demarcated parterres, Swensen lets her imagination move over them until they become the source of a different sublime from that which the Romantics shivered at as they contemplated the Alps or the ocean—a geometric sublime, comparable to what the advanced metaphysician sees in a well-formed equation or proof.

73. Jenny Boully, *The Body: An Essay* (Slope Editions, 2002)

The Body is subtitled "An Essay," a gesture I didn't give much thought to until I heard Dinty Moore, in a lecture on the unfolding wonders and potentialities of "creative nonfiction," hail Boully's book as being on the cutting edge of this institutionally emergent genre. And then I noted that Boully in her acknowledgments thanks not only the poets John Matthias and Robert Kelly, but the doyen of the "lyric essay," John D'Agata. So maybe, I begin to think, there's something important going on in this generic gesture.

The Body consists of a series of footnotes to an absent text. A large part of how the book works is the reader's ongoing attempt to figure out precisely *what* that text might consist of: is it a memoir (as many of the first person notes seem to indicate)? is it a slightly salacious literary biography? is it a work of linguistic philosophy (references to Levinas and Derrida)? is it the history of a particular play (notes about varying "productions")? is it some combination of all of these things, and a great deal more?

Ultimately, the "text" to which *The Body* furnishes the footnotes must be as fragmentary, non-linear, and wide-ranging as those footnotes themselves. (The notes section of Nabokov's *Pale Fire*, and even the notes to *The Waste Land*, make documents far more coherent than *The Body*.) I like this book. I like its sense of mystery and inconsequence, its flashes of humor and raw emotion—but I find myself reading it not as an *essay*, but as *poetry*. That is, if one places *The Body* among the works of the post-avant written in the past 30 years, even in its most radical formal gestures it seems to be working within a clear tradition. If one reads it among essays, however, it seems quite blindingly radical, out on the very limits of the genre. And I wonder if that isn't precisely the position the writer (the poet? the essayist?) wanted to claim in the subtitle.

74. Susan Stewart, *The Forest* (University of Chicago Press, 1995)

A kind of effortless mastery to much of this book, and a deep interest in *interesting things* quite apart from the poet's own sensibility, which I appreciate—the embryology of "The Desert 1990–1993," the Biblical rewriting of "Lamentations." "Medusa Anthology," which revolves around Géricault's grand *Raft of the Medusa*, is the great set-piece, but for my tastes it ends on a far too lyrical, conclusive note—as do too many of the poems. I think I like the more ambiguous, fragmentary works of Part I, "Phantom," better than the more accomplished longer pieces of "Cinder," the second part. But there's much to admire throughout the book, even if Stewart in her more traditionally formalist moments isn't my cuppa.

75. Donald Revell, *Thief of Strings* (Alice James, 2007)

I read Revell in a kind of enraptured haze, I'm so taken with the odd combination of his poetry: a lovely, consistent lyricism, a mild, very American surrealism, an entranced eye for the unfolding details of the (especially natural) world, closely tied in with a genial piety. If Geoffrey Hill is a High Church Anglican Prophetic poet, and Susan Howe an Antinomian Calvinist poet, then Revell is a *Franciscan* poet. And that's a compliment.

76. Susan Stewart, *Columbarium* (University of Chicago Press, 2003)

A book of "first things"—between the bookends of four longish poems on the four Empedoclean elements—air, fire, water, earth—a series of shorter poems on various themes, arranged from A to Z. The elements of which we are made and among which we live, and the twenty-six glyphs by which we comprehend and express them. A curious blending of the pre-Sokratic and the high classical (Virgil's *Georgics* one touchstone). As always in Stewart's work, an almost obsessive, loving regard for the evidence of the senses. An impressive range of forms in the alphabetic section, most of them ad hoc and gracefully realized.

77. Susan Stewart, *Red Rover* (University of Chicago Press, 2008)

More spare than the poems of *Columbarium* and *The Forest*, less of the lush lyricism of those volumes. The contemporary seems to nag the poet, a humming distraction or a moral quandary continually pulling her away from a contemplation of first things—either the immediate data of the natural world, or the spiritual, martial, and erotic matter of the Middle Ages and classical antiquity.

78. John Godfrey, *City of Corner* (Wave Books, 2008)

I need to read more of Godfrey, I think. This collection and *Midnight on Your Left*, from two decades ago, are all I know of his work, but I like both of them very much. Very much—overwhelmingly—an urban poet, a poet of the subway and the city streets and the city nightclubs. An alert, almost aching sensuality, scented with taxi and bus exhaust and the New York summer perfume of rotting garbage—which doesn't one bit subtract from the poems' fundamental sexiness, or disguise the thread of longing and affection that runs throughout the volume.

79. Allen Grossman, *Descartes' Loneliness* (New Directions, 2007)

As befitting the title, a book of meditative poems, on first things and (often) last things, death, conclusion. Scenes of instruction ("the long schoolroom" is Grossman's figure for the poet's vocation), not untouched by the erotics of learning on which Anne Carson and Guy Davenport have written so eloquently. One is reminded of the late Yeats, and occasionally of William Bronk, though Grossman, for me at least, is a far more genial poet than Bronk. Bronk stares unblinkingly into the abyss and issues dour reports; Grossman dances on the edge, aware of his solitude but continually reaching out and blowing kisses to his companions.

80. Stacy Szymaszek, *Emptied of All Ships* (Litmus Press, 2008)

One's first unavoidable thought—given the marine imagery, the occasional typographical flourishes—is of Mallarmé's *Un coup de dés*, extended over 70-odd pages. But Mallarmé's is an immediate, one-time-only shipwreck, a single long statement or canvas (a Turner?), while Szymaszek's is a whole voyage, a circumnavigation, a Hakluyt of sailings-forth—touching islands, sea battles, reading French novels in the cabin, tattooing one's hand with a bartered needle, the implacable boredom of shipboard. I've never been on a voyage longer than the Scotland-to-Belfast ferry (well, I once crossed the Atlantic, but I was only three months old at the time and don't remember, though my parents tell me I was blessedly immune to seasickness) but I've read Melville and Dana. Szymaszek, in a radically different idiom—short-lined, spare, rich in allusion—has written a voyage as redolent of the ocean as *White-Jacket* or *Two Years Before the Mast*.

81. Forrest Gander, *The Blue Rock Collection* (Salt, 2004)

I was unaware that Forrest Gander had a degree in geology, but it makes perfect sense, given his sharp eye for minerals. *The Blue Rock Collection* is a something of a mineralogically-slanted "greatest hits" from Gander's previously published books, poems complemented by Rikki Ducornet's drawings of rocks, twigs, birds' skulls. "A Poetic Essay on Creation, Evolution, and Imagination" is a fine, plainspoken laying-out of Gander's poetics and the ethos behind Lost Roads Books, the excellent small press he and C. D. Wright edit.

82. Janet Holmes, *The Ms of My Kin* (Shearsman, 2009)

I'd begun to get intimations that Ronald Johnson's technique in erasing swatches of *Paradise Lost* to make his own *Radi Os* was, thirty years on, beginning to get picked up as a viable, repeatable compositional technique, rather than a one-off tour de force. But Holmes's *Ms of My Kin*, an "erasure" of two years' worth of *The Poems of Emily Dickinson*, is the first full-length volume of such work, post-Johnson, I've encountered.

Holmes gives the technique a twist: where Johnson's erasure of Milton, much like Zukofsky's earlier slice-up in "A"-14, ends up producing a series of highly disjunctive, vividly fragmentary poems that fit snugly within Johnson's already established obsessions with light, the eye, natural processes, etc., Holmes provides a final note linking her own Dickinson excavations (pointedly, from poems composed over the first two years of the Civil War) with the World Trade Center attacks, the invasion of Afghanistan, and the debacle in Iraq—IEDs, Abu Ghraib, Guantánamo, the whole blood-boltered business.

The project, then, becomes a series of dramatic monologues spoken by various figures of the last eight years, from Al-Qaeda terrorists to American torturers to Bush himself, and by a voice one might identify with the poet herself—alternatively angry, bewildered, and despairing at the Republic's mad wrong turnings. There's a tension here that sits uneasily with me: where *Radi Os* was composed (like Blake's illuminated books or Tom Phillips's *Humument*) on the level of the page, the page as icon, as it were, Holmes tends to run her discourse from page to page, at the same time preserving the line positions of the often solitary remaining words. It feels, at times, as though Dickinson has become a resource within which the words for preëxisting statements have been found, rather than a text within which new and unexpected poems have been discovered.

Perhaps that's just a function of my saturation in Johnson; probably, I need to live with Holmes's book a bit longer to get used to her particular take on the poetics of erasure. But at any rate, I can say right now that the poems of *The Ms of My Kin* are powerful, sometimes funny, and often very moving.

83. David Mutschlecner, *Sign* (Ahsahta, 2007)

I've never been inclined one way or another in regards to "religious" or spiritual poetry, though I've read my share of Herbert, Donne, and Milton, grappled with Hopkins and David Jones, and more recently enjoyed the work of Donald Revell and Peter O'Leary. It seems somehow appropriate that I paused at the midpoint of Dante's *Paradiso* to read David Mutchlecner's *Sign*. I must confess—the ceremonies and theology of Roman Catholicism are an alien country to me, brought up as I was in an icon-smashing, bare-pewed Protestantism. But I'm much moved by *Sign*, by Mutschlecner's quiet, spare, syntactically straightforward poems of spiritual experience. These are the poems that an ascetic desert Father might write, if he came in the aesthetic mode of Robert Creeley, Theodore Enslin, and Ronald Johnson. The final long sequence, "Poems for the Feast of Corpus Christi," makes the mass come alive for me more vividly than anyone except David Jones himself.

84. Caroline Bergvall, *Goan Atom* (Krupskaya, 2001)

Zowie! A more rambunctious, high-spirited, madly inventive book hasn't come my way in ages. The Brits, I've gathered, are rightly suspicious of that squishy term the "postmodern," and those among their interesting writers who take the trouble to label what they're up to tend rather toward the label "late modernist." If Bergvall—a British/Norwegian/French poet based in the U. K.—'s treading a modernist path, late or otherwise, however, it's by no means the familiar Pound-Williams-Olson idiom of much of the New American Poetry, but rather some unholy, crystal-meth-fueled mixture of Stein, Jarry, Duchamp, Dada, and Russian Futurist *Zaum*. Voices drop in and out of dialect, letters spill over the page, words break up and reform before one's eyes. It's all about sex and puppets, I think, but I'm far from sure, and don't really care: it makes a lovely, exhilarating noise. Is Bergvall the Derek Bailey of poetry?

85. Norman Finkelstein, *Scribe* (Dos Madres, 2009)

Finkelstein's last full-length volume, *Passing Over* (Marsh Hawk, 2007), was something of a digression for those of us watching the growth and progression of his career, consisting as it did of poems for the most part composed before the three volumes of his simultaneously rich and spare sequence *Track*. *Scribe*, his first real post-*Track* collection, marks the moment when one can clearly begin setting Finkelstein in the same rank as his self-proclaimed masters, among them William Bronk, Robert Duncan, and Michael Palmer (who contributes a fine blurb). This is a volume for which blustery superlatives seem inappropriate, for the pleasures and mysteries of these poems are subtle, insinuative ones—the riddling, ritualistic anabasis of "Drones and Chants" (the volume's first section), the quirky assemblages of "Collages," which draw on everything from fairy tales to Jewish mysticism to celtic ballads.

The real heart of the volume is the last section, "An Assembly," a series of poems playing off of the architect Christopher Alexander's *A Pattern Language* (1977), something of a "generative grammar" for the design of humanized living spaces. Finkelstein takes Alexander's descriptions of various habitant spheres—the marriage bed, the sidewalk café, the spiritual center—as jumping-off points for poems that are quiet meditations on the places in which we lead—or *ought to* lead—our lives. And the physical spaces of which Alexander writes—rooms, houses, halls, arcades—become in Finkelstein's hands a series of metaphorical spaces: the space of consciousness, the interpersonal space of a marriage, the shifting and interlocking spaces of the poems themselves, in their sequence. "An Awakening" is a mysterious but deeply good-natured work, and—like so much of Finkelstein's poetry, which has never surrendered the Romantic vision of poetry as ultimately redemptive—a deeply *utopian* one.

86. Tony Lopez, *Covers* (Salt Publishing, 2007)

Covers, the dust jacket tells us, is a "deeply derivative" work—derivative, not in the sense of being imitative of other poets, but of drawing its language—the *whole* of its language, "unencumbered by any poeticizing feedback," Bob Perelman says in a blurb—from outside sources. One can recognize bits and pieces of other poems, newspaper reports and copy, various types of journalese and essayese, even a series of fragments from papers delivered at a Pound conference. It's all, oddly enough, concatenated in a very traditional manner, at least to these ears. Lopez is neither a Flarfiste, mining his sources for outrageousness and the shock of the hyper-banal, nor a conceptualist, hewing closely to a method—though there are traces of both of these approaches in *Covers*. The poems here have clear shapes (is this no more than a readerly impression?), and for the most part clear, even emphatic, closure. Even in a hyper-late-modernist mode of radical collage, Lopez preserves the ancient functions of delight and instruction—or at least *laus et vituperatio*.

87. John Wilkinson, *Down to Earth* (Salt, 2008)

I'm very keen on John Wilkinson's work, though I'm sensible as well of the possible criticism that Wilkinson—now a professor at Notre Dame but before that (to his credit) a career non-academic, working for the U.K. mental health service for some 30 years—and yes, I suppose, a "Cambridge poet"—represents one of the purest examples of J. H. Prynne's influence on contemporary English poetry. But hey, I adore Prynne just short of idolatry, and am happy to read Prynne-*werk* of any sort, whether by J. H. P. or not.

At any rate, I don't think that's a fair assessment of Wilkinson's work, anyway. The early books, certainly, show many Prynneian (Prynnesque?) marks—an extreme sentence by sentence disjunctiveness, a prickly and often esoteric, technical vocabulary, the continual subversion of semantic sense within the framework of conventional (if often attenuated) syntax. But Wilkinson's last few books, particularly the two he's produced since landing on this side of the Atlantic—*Lake Shore Drive* and *Down to Earth*—show him moving in a far more—er—down to earth direction. The freshness of language is still there, along with the often arresting shifts of register and a kind of agonized intellectual and emotional intensity, but they're integrated quite explicitly with a deep engagement with the contemporary—with geopolitics and American politics, with the fracturing of the environment, with the banal and marvelous American scene in general. If anything, in *Down to Earth* I'm struck by the precise *formality* of Wilkinson's syntax: at times I'm wondering if I'm reading the works of a Donald Davie late-converted to the avant-garde. He might take that as an insult; I mean it as nothing but compliment.

88. Joel Bettridge, *Presocratic Blues* (Chax, 2009)

One of my favorite college assignments of all time was a take-home midterm in Nick Smith's "History of Philosophy" ("Part I: Pre-Socratics through Plato") course back at Virginia Tech. Nick handed out an unidentified pre-Socratic fragment (he'd written it himself, of course), and our assignment was to identify its "author" on the basis of doctrine, style, or whatever logical clues we could follow. (Hint: It's not by Pythagoras, who left no extant writings.)

I think I got an "A" on that one, and have remained more than mildly fascinated by the pre-Socratics ever since. (My copy of Kirk and Raven is on the verge of disintegrating.) I love it that some of them wrote their philosophy in verse—which is part of what gives Joel Bettridge's project, a mash-up of pre-Socratic philosophy and classic American blues, a kind of air of inevitability (why didn't I think of that?) even as it comes as a complete surprise.

Nifty poems these, constantly surprising and amusing, divided into "Testamonia"—poems about various pre-Socratics overlaid with various blues figures ("Diogenes and Stagolee in a Punch-Up," "At cards Hippocrates and Blind Willie Johnson ...") and "Hollers," poems attributed to various pre-Socratics, in which the mysterious totalities of their philosophies are juxtaposed with the affective immediacies and repetitive structures of classic blues. It's got a great beat and you can dance to it, and (to quote—is it Spinal Tap?) it makes you *think*.

89. Gary Snyder, *Axe Handles* (North Point, 1983)

It's been years since I've read a Snyder book. I'd forgotten what a tonic his straightforward delivery and terse, quasi-Asian lyricism can be. I can live without the joyful ecocelebration—the last poem ends "one ecosystem / in diversity / under the sun / With joyful interpenetration for all"—not that I don't sympathize with the Thoreauvian impulse behind so much of the verse, it's just that—well, maybe it all feels a bit too Sixties-ish optimistic. I find it hard to write about nature, or even to look at nature, without being overwhelmed with a stomach-bottoming sense of foreboding and even guilt at what we've made of poor old Mater Gaia, now circling the drain. But Snyder's at his best when he's chronicling the intense pleasures he gets out of the *grain* of everyday living, the daily grind of dropping the kids off for their ride to school, trying to keep the raccoons out of the refrigerator at night, drinking and eating.

90. Geraldine Monk, *Selected Poems* (Salt, 2003)

I already knew *Interregnum*, the centerpiece volume of this big selection of Monk's work, a snazzy recounting of the trial and execution of the East Lancastershire Pendle Witches in 1612. Good stuff—Monk's seventeenth-century witches tend to blur into twentieth-century bikers, anarchists, crusties, and other British anti-establishment types, and her language is always muscular and surprising. The four post-*Interregnum* collections in *Selected Poems* show Monk moving in interesting directions. The early work is a bit too druggy and Wiccan for my taste at times; the later is more satisfyingly weird, breaking up and morphing words on the phonemic level, circling around verbal motifs and repeated cadences. Oddly enough, I find it far more emotionally immediate than the earlier things.

91. Ray DiPalma, *Raik* (Roof, 1989)

This is procedural poetry on some level, or at least it takes the notion of *form* to whole new levels of rigor. Each poem, that is, is composed of evenly-spaced lines: sixteen characters, or thirty-two characters, or whatever. Typeset, obviously, in a crunky Courier-like font in order to preserve ye olde typewritere look, but you get used to that in a page or two. I'd love to know how DiPalma did it: on the computer, with a Courier font? on a real live typewriter? by hand, on graph paper? I'd also love to figure out the numerology behind the various poems, which come in all sorts of even stanzas and line-lengths. It's something of a spit in the face to the whole notion of the page as field of composition, the typewriter as "scoring" the voice (Cummings, L. Z., Olson, Duncan), but in a good way: for what's amazing here is the richness and energy of DiPalma's lines, the way he manages to shovel in all sorts of linguistic registers and subject-matter. The poems here range from spare Creeley- or Zukofsky-esque lyrics to dense philosophical meditations to Steinian round-songs. And all in these teeny, über-constrained little boxes. The sort of book that sends me to the keyboard and notebooks to *write*, and that's praise.

92. Stephen Collis, *The Commons* (Talonbooks, 2008)

This is the second installment of a sequence?—network?—work begun in *Anarchive* (North Star Books, 2005), and whose overriding title is "The Barricades Project." A kind of reinventing, reinterpretation, reanimation of various past radicalisms—in this case the flash points are Winstanley's Levellers, ca. 1649; Henry David Thoreau; John Clare; and the various Lake Poets in general. I have enormous sympathy and interest in Collis's project, not least in how it overlaps with my own "Anarchy for the U.K." sequence (much of which appears in *Anarchy* [Spuyten Duyvil, 2003]). and I envy the extent to which Collis has gone beyond Duncan and Howe—his most obvious precursors—in thinking about the literary heritage as a kind of poetic "commons" as yet unenclosed, open not to appropriation but to principled, shared use.

93. Majorie Welish, *Word Group* (Coffee House, 2004)

This one's a knockout. It's all rich, and strange, and suggestive, but the parts that stick with me most insistently are the sixteen-section "Textile," which "weaves" a long poem, at least in the early bits, out of repeated phrases and structures as warp and woof. Best is "Delight Instruct" (as in Horace, get it?), a long poem which both dissects and rebuilds some Penguin volume of art history—not its *contents*, but its *form*—laying bare both the ordinariness and the strangeness of that oddest of information-bearing objects, the bound codex. *Word Group* is saturated throughout with evidences of Welish's other lives as visual artist and art critic. Poems both painterly and conceptual at once.

94. Karla Kelsey, *Knowledge, Forms, The Aviary* (Ahsahta, 2006)

A fine instance of the period style in obliquity, descending one suspects less from a reading of Michael Palmer than from a sustained engagement with Jorie Graham's mid-period work. Kelsey's writing is lean and surprising, many lines little short of amazing. But I can't help feeling that the package as a whole, from the big white spaces of the pages, the breathless gravity of the lines, the intensity of the jacket photo, even the book's overall design—is all too familiar. Kelsey largely redeems herself in the book's last section, where the focus shifts from individual epistemology to the "polis," the intersubjective social realm. And none too soon.

Is subjectivity the only thing worth reading about? Has today's period style merely re-inscribed the Romantic Ideology (cf. Jerome McGann) within a framework of vaguely post-avant, paratactic formal gestures?

95. Jorie Graham, *The Errancy* (Ecco, 1997)

Is this what one calls "mid-period" Graham? At any rate, she's retreated from the more extravagant formal experiments of *The End of Beauty* and *Materialism* to a more recognizable, if still extravagant, first-person-centered subjectivity here. I can't gainsay the brilliance of the writing here, the endlessly proliferating excess of metaphor and striking language, the lyrical phrases that seem to pour out as if from an unstoppable cornucopia. But must it always, always be a mere tracing of the poet's brilliant and sensitive processing of the world? It's as if Graham's sensibility is one great open wound of perception and thought, constantly aching out a stream of language in response to the world's phenomena. "The river," at least, speaks to the poet in terms of self-recognition: "*why do you hurry to drown yourself in me / its flashing waves laugh-up, / why do you expect constant attention / why your eagerness for self-creation, self-explanation—/ what would you explain ...*" Kelsey, in contrast, is a model of restrained thought, a careful sorting-out of the rush of particulars in the sensorium; Graham is the rush itself.

96. Tod Thilleman, *Root-Cellar to Riverine* (Spuyten Duyvil, Meeting Eyes Bindery, 2009)

Tod Thilleman's been running Spuyten Duyvil as long as I can remember, and he's published some memorable books indeed: the best, for my money, the three volumes of Norman Finkelstein's big *Track* project and Peter O'Leary's luminous *Watchfulness*. (Spuyten Duyvil's also keeping important things of Michael Heller's in print, and, yes, they published—and did a very nice job of—my own *Anarchy*.) So ashes of shame on my head for never having explored Tod's own poetry before *Root-Cellar to Riverine* turned up in my mailbox. It's a quirky little book—a single long poem in something like sixty twelve-line, very small-format pages. Thilleman has a music all his own, sometimes lyrical, sometimes dissonant; pretty consistently surprising. I'll admit the word "root-cellar" always sets me thinking of WCW's "cat" poem—you know, the one with the jam-closet and so forth. But *Root-Cellar* is very un-Williamsesque: more an assertion—nay, a demonstration—that ruminative, considerative poetry is still possible. You've got to admire Thilleman's ability to leap from the jars in the cellar to the meaning of life; and it doesn't at all hurt that the poem to my ear's shot through with echoes of *Briggflatts*.

I'm glad to see SD back on deck, after some heavy weather, with a (relatively) new(ish) poetry imprint, Meeting Eyes Bindery. A couple more things on my shelf I'm looking forward to opening: Richard Blevins's *Captivity Narratives*, which looks like precisely the sort of history- and text-based thing (Stephen Collis, Susan Howe, Olson) that gets me excited; and a twofer, *Breathing Bolaño*, which pairs (in different print orientations) Thilleman's *Breathing* and selections from Blevins's *Corrido of Bolaño*, along with a chunk of the two poets' correspondence.

97. Richard Blevins, *Captivity Narratives* (Spuyten Duyvil, Meeting Eyes Bindery, 2009)

To get past the obvious: Blevins is an Olsonian, a real live Olsonian—he took over editing the Olson/Creeley correspondence after George Butterick's death. As poets, Olsonians (my limited experience has shown me) tend to have a certain repertoire of moves that Olson has made familiar : an obsession with history, a tendency to splice documents into the work itself, a self-reflexive awareness of their own position as poem-makers, even as they write. Blevins has all of these (as does, say, Susan Howe). What he doesn't share with the Big Man is his (liberating?) formal sprawl, his taste for the cosmic and the anciently recondite—the Big Gesture, sometimes registered in geological epochs.

Captivity Narratives is a pair of intense investigations into a couple of figures with whom I was not at all familiar before cracking the book: the photographer Fred Holland Day (1864–1933), one of the first advocates for photography as a "fine" art, and the maker of mysterious, often homoerotic pictures; and Adelaide Crapsey (1878–1914), a poet whose work I was vaguely aware of, but whose fame has largely waned since the days Carl Sandburg championed her. Blevins reads these two figures' relative obscurity as their own versions of "captivity." His poems are as much about the researching—sometimes down to the details of library visits and overnight travel—as they are about Day and Crapsey themselves, but the effect is to position Blevins's own work something of a (necessarily interminable) detective story. (The biographer in me finds this irresistible.) I'm particularly taken, among the stretches of short-lined verse, rambling narrative prose, and sheer notebook-entry fragments, to find Blevins casting his impressions of Crapsey into her own invented form, the "cinquain."

98. Tom Mandel, *Four Strange Books* (Gaz, 1990)

Elias Bickerman's classic study of anomalous Hebrew Bible texts, *Four Strange Books of the Bible* (1985), focuses on Jonah, Daniel, Koheleth ("Ecclesiastes" for you Christian-types), and Esther. It's easy to see why he calls them "strange": Jonah is not a book of prophecy, but a kind of Three Stooges parody of the Isaiahan prophetic call; Daniel is a strange, back-dated collage of various tall tales and prophecies; Koheleth advances a depressing stoic philosophy that seems at odds with much of what the rest of the Hebrew Bible advocates; and Esther is a fairy tale that manages not even to mention the Hebrew deity.

Perhaps on some rereading I'll figure out a bit better precisely how Tom Mandel's wonderful *Four Strange Books* plays off of Bickerman. Right now I'm just reveling in the pleasure of this late-discovered (for me) classic. Mandel may at the moment be becoming my favorite of the *Grand Piano* poets (I read his *To the Congnoscenti* over the holidays in something like transfixed delight). He has an unerring eye for the movement of the everyday, a stern sense of juxtaposition, and a wonderful knack of shifting diction. The opening of the title poem, "Four Strange Books," which plays on various phrases of biblical and archaeological resonance, is one of the most striking, hieratic moments in poetry in the last two decades:

> A tract was sealed in the catacomb of cylinders
> by three youths called Ejection, Sacrifice,
> and Trellis. To a skeptic the treatise speaks
> of things still possible.

> What it says will never do. If they reach
> toward me I will collapse. Touch me then
> my shoulder with strengthened lips; that
> man was swallowed!

99. Douglas Rothschild, *Theogony* (subpress, 2009)

Imagine Frank O'Hara as a dyed-in-the-wool, place-saturated, native New Yorker, who takes all five boroughs as his home ground, all their parks, neighborhoods, bodegas, apartment developments, social distinctions as his purview, rather than a Boston-bred artsy Manhattanite. Then imagine his "I do this I do that" poetics, with all their camp humor and delight in popular culture intact, stripped of their art world in-crowd talk and surrealist flights and focused on the immediate state of mind of the *real* New Yorker (continually worried about the rent, about what new enormities the mayor's about to perpetrate). Then put him, equipped with an angry socio-political bullshit detector, into the most savagely repressive and bewildering moment in recent American history—the post-September 11th morass. Then set him to work jotting down poems that angrily and painfully pin down the cost to the American psyche of our Republican masters' reactions to the World Trade Center destruction.

That's the long sequence "The Minor Arcana," something of a masterpiece of making the political personal in an age of electronic media. But all of the sections of *Theogony* are quirky, moving, and deeply impressive, as strongly rooted in *polis* as Olson's rambles around Dogtown—and a hell of a lot funnier.

100. Julie Carr, *100 Notes on Violence* (Ahsahta, 2009)

A beautiful, large-format book with some very ugly things inside, a kind of tour of the American culture of hurt, with special attention to domestic violence against women and the consequences of keeping handguns around the house. Carr has a delicate ear, and her segments are often kinds of mobiles of suspended syntax and thoughtful music (that music, interestingly enough, is often *country* music), pressed up against sections of dense statistics (gun ownership, death rates, etc.) or intimidating text-blocks presenting the roiling insides of people in the grip of "vengeance" or other varieties of Homeric anger. What's most initially compelling, however, beyond the formal variety of the 100 "notes," is the degree to which Carr speaks in a *personal* voice; her narrative of her own upbringing and its emotional violence, her lyrics of maternal protection, have an stark attraction that sets all of the book's news-derived material into a frame of emotional immediacy. Of course, she may be making up the "personal" bits—I don't know; and I don't really care: they *work*, they take the poem beyond reportage and ventriloquizing into a space of scary realism.

(Now that I think about it, the book *100 Notes on Violence* most resembles for me at the moment is Rukeyser's *Book of the Dead*. Go figure.)

[This winds up the "100 poem-books" project that I so sanguinely began a bit over (gulp) two years ago, expecting to dash through it in maybe fourteen months. It's not that I didn't read that many slim (and fat) volumes of contemporary (and older) verse in the year after I started blogging books and putting them under this rubric, it's just that, well, there were lots that I didn't feel were really worth blogging about; and there were others that just so knocked me out that I dithered around, thinking about what I'd write, until something else came up; and there were times when I just plain got lazy. So sue me. You can have your money back.]

Index to "100 Poem-Books"

[*The poets and titles are indexed to entry numbers*]

Alexander, Charles, *Near or Random Acts* 68
Armantrout, Rae, *Next Life* 4
Arnold, Elizabeth, *Civilization* 27; *The Reef* 54
Ashbery, John, and Joe Brainard, *The Vermont Notebook* 46
Barnett, Anthony, *Poem About Music* 25
Beowulf (trans. Seamus Heaney) 16
Bergvall, Caroline, *Goan Atom* 84
Bettridge, Joel, *Presocratic Blues* 88
Blevins, Richard, *Captivity Narratives* 97
Bouchard, Daniel, *Sound Swarms and Other Poems* 32
Boully, Jenny, *The Body: An Essay* 73
Bronk, William, *Manifest; And Furthermore* 28
Browne, Laynie, *Rebecca Letters* 2
Carr, Julie, *100 Notes on Violence* 100
cheek, cris, *The Church—The School—The Beer* 21
Cole, Peter, *Things on Which I've Stumbled* 69
Collis, Stephen, *The Commons* 92
Clover, Joshua, *The Totality for Kids* 56
DiPalma, Ray, *Raik* 91
Donahue, Joseph, *Before Creation* 65; *World Well Broken* 66
Duncan, Robert, *Roots and Branches* 5
Felix, Joel, *Monaural* 30
Finkelstein, Norman, *Scribe* 85
Forché, Carolyn, *Gathering the Tribes* 51
Foust, Graham, *As in Every Deafness* 36; *Necessary Stranger* 37
Fuller, William, *Sadly* 53; *Watchword* 22
Gander, Forrest, *The Blue Rock Collection* 81
Giscombe, C. S., *Prairie Style* 62
Gizzi, Peter, *The Outernationale* 40; *Periplum and other Poems, 1987–1992* 63; *Some Values of Landscape and Weather* 39

Godfrey, John, *City of Corner* 78; *Midnight on Your Left* 8
Graham, Jorie, *The Errancy* 96
Graham, K. Lorraine, *Terminal Humming* 35
Grossman, Allen, *Descartes' Loneliness* 79
Guest, Barbara, *The Red Gaze* 48
Halsey, Alan, *Fit to Print* (with Karen Mac Cormack) 3; *Not Everything Remotely: Selected Poems 1978–2005* 45
Hejinian, Lyn, *The Beginner* 43; *Slowly* 38
Holmes, Janet, *Humanophone* 71; *The Ms of My Kin* 82
Howald, Isabelle Baladine, *Secret of Breath* 55
Howard, Richard, *Without Saying* 34
Howe, Susan, *Souls of the Labadie Tract* 7
Jarnot, Lisa, *Black Dog Songs* 50; *Night Scenes* 24
Johnston, Devin, *Sources* 12
Kelsey, Karla, *Knowledge, Forms, The Aviary* 94
Kleinzahler, August, *The Strange Hours Travelers Keep* 9
Kyger, Joanne, *Not Veracruz* 41
Lopez, Tony, *Covers* 86
Mac Cormack, Karen, *Fit to Print* (with Alan Halsey) 3
Mackey, Nathaniel, *Splay Anthem* 6
Mandell, Tom, *Four Strange Books* 98
Marvell, Andrew, *The Complete Poems* 60
Matthias, John, *Kedging: New Poems* 42
Menashe, Samuel, *New and Selected Poems* 14
Middleton, Christopher, *Tankard Cat* 18; *The Tenor on Horseback* 23
Monk, Geraldine, *Selected Poems* 90; *She Kept Birds* 33
Moxley, Jennifer, *The Line* 57
Mutschlecner, David, *Sign* 83
Nielson, Melanie, *Natural Facts* 10
Novalis, *Hymns to the Night* (trans. Dick Higgins) 13
Pickard, Tom, *Ballad of Jamie Allan* 20
Portugal, Anne, *Quisite Moment* 67

Pritchett, Patrick, *Antiphonal* 11
Raffel, Burton (trans.), *Pure Pagan: Seven Centuries of Greek Poems and Fragments* 17
Revell, Donald, *Thief of Strings* 75
Roberson, Ed, *Atmosphere Conditions* 1
Robinson, Elizabeth, *Apostrophe* 19
Robinson, Kit, *The Champagne of Concrete* 70; *Ice Cubes* 61
Rothschild, Douglas, *Theogony* 99
Shapiro, David, *To An Idea: A Book of Poems* 59
Silliman, Ron, *The Age of Huts (compleat)* 52
Snyder, Gary, *Axe Handles* 89
Sophocles, *Ajax* (trans. John Tipton) 15
Stein, Gertrude, *Tender Buttons* 64
Stewart, Susan, *Columbarium* 76; *The Forest* 74; *Red Rover* 77
Swensen, Cole, *Ours* 72
Szymaszek, Stacy, *Emptied of All Ships* 80
Taggart, John, *There Are Birds* 58
Thilleman, Tod, *Root-Cellar to Riverine* 96
Tipton, John, *Four Fables* 29
Toscano, Rodrigo, *Platform* 44
Vincent, Stephen, *Walking Theory* 26
Watson, Craig, *True News* 49
Welish, Marjorie, *Word Group* 93
Wilkinson, John, *Down to Earth* 87
Wordsworth, William, and Samuel Taylor Coleridge, *Lyrical Ballads* 31
Wright, Jay, *Music's Mask and Measure* 47

About the Author

Mark Scroggins was born in an American military hospital in Frankfurt, West Germany, as—quite coincidentally—Theodor Adorno prepared to deliver lectures on "History and Freedom" across town at the Institut für Sozialforschung at the Johann Wolfgang Goethe-Universität. He spent his childhood in various military bases in West Germany; Syracuse, New York; Monterey, California; San Angelo, Texas; Murray, Kentucky—before settling in Clarksville, Tennessee, where he graduated from high school. After studying literature and philosophy at Virginia Tech, he did graduate work in English and creative writing at Cornell University, and eventually joined the English Department at Florida Atlantic University in Boca Raton.

Scroggins's early scholarly work centered on the American modernist poet Louis Zukofsky, culminating in the critical biography *The Poem of a Life* (Shoemaker & Hoard, 2007), which was a *New York Times Book Review* "editor's choice" and a *Choice* "Outstanding Academic Title of the Year." Scroggins has also written essays and reviews on many modernist and contemporary writers, appearing in such collections as *A History of Modernist Poetry* (Cambridge University Press, 2015), *The Cambridge History of American Poetry, The Oxford History of the Novel in English, The Cambridge Companion to American Poetry Since 1945, A Companion to Poetic Genres*, and *The Cambridge Companion to Modernist Poetry*, and in journals, most notably, essays in *Parnassus: Poetry in Review*. Much of this work was collected in *Intricate Thicket: Reading Late Modernist Poetries* (University of Alabama Press, 2015).

Scroggins wrote iambic pentameter at Virginia Tech under the "New Formalist" Wyatt Prunty; his MFA thesis at Cornell was directed by A. R. Ammons. His first collection of poems, *Anarchy* (Spuyten Duyvil, 2003), was followed by *Torture Garden: Naked City Pastorelles* (The Cultural Society, 2011) and *Red Arcadia* (Shearsman, 2012). A fourth collection, *Pressure Dressing*, is forthcoming.

Most recently, Scroggins has returned to an interest in fantasy and science fiction, publishing the monograph *Michael Moorcock: Fiction, Fantasy and the World's Pain* (McFarland, 2015). His current projects: a book on the aesthetic and epistemological issues at play in writing literary and philosophical biography; an essay on aesthetic and social implications of the instability of texts (with special attention to Emily Dickinson, Susan Howe, and Robert E. Howard); a book on the fragment; and a wide-ranging study of the influence of the Victorian art and social critic John Ruskin.

www.ingramcontent.com/pod-product-compliance
Lightning Source LLC
Chambersburg PA
CBHW020330170426
43200CB00006B/333